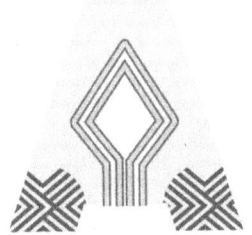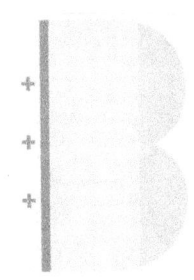

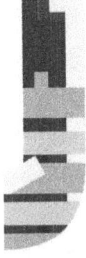

JABULANI
MEANS
REJOICE

DICTIONARY OF SOUTH AFRICAN NAMES

HUMZILE SIMELANE KALUMBA

Jabulani Means Rejoice
A dictionary of South African names, 2nd edition

Text © Phumzile Simelane Kalumba
Cover artwork: Jacqui Stecher
Cover design: Jacqui Stecher and Fire & Lion
Edited by Colleen Crawford Cousins and Karen Jennings
Book Design: Fire & Lion
First published by Modjaji Books in 2012
This edition published in 2018

modjajibooks.co.za

ISBN (Print): 978-1-928215-49-3

All rights reserved. No part of this book may be reproduced or transmitted in any form or by any electronic or mechanical means, including photocopying and recording, or any other information storage or retrieval system, without written permission from the publisher.

Dedication

To my mother Mrs J.A Simelane, whose name we changed from *Jabsile* (disappointing) to *Jabulisile* (the one who brings joy): for she has been nothing but a joy to us. And to my Dad Muzikawulahlwa, Kawaliwa, futhi Kawungcwatshwa ngithi Mpembe elikhulu Mnguni wasebuhleni, Ngiyambonga uNkulunkulu ngawe Nkonyane yeNkosi.

Introduction

Nelson Rholihlahla Mandela commented on his African name, Rholihlahla ('pulling the branch') – a phrase in Xhosa meaning 'troublemaker' or 'someone who has gone through a lot of trouble' – which was given to him by his father. The branch referred to is the gate of the cattle kraal; if you pulled it aside, the cattle would run out, endangering crops and people. 'But,' comments Nelson Mandela, 'in later years, friends and relatives would ascribe to my birth name the many storms I have both caused and weathered.'

Naming is important. Current moves in South Africa to rename provinces, cities, roads, buildings and rivers attempt to ensure that all South Africans feel they belong.

How did we lose our beautiful traditional names, and how can we reclaim them?

During the era of colonialism in South Africa, Christian missionaries from Europe built the first schools, hospitals and churches. A new convert to Christianity was required to take a 'Christian' name. School administrators gave a child a new name, known as a 'school name' on registration day, the first day of a child's school career. Only baptism or school names were used as first names on official documents. One's African name was only used at home, and became known as *igama lasekhaya* (Nguni). The educated would be addressed by their school name, also known as their official name: *igama lasesitifiketini* (Nguni). With the inferiority complex instilled by colonialism, the use of African names became shameful. They were looked down upon as exclusively for the unlearned.

My grandmother told us many stories when we were growing up. A story that was close to her heart was about the herd of cattle she left in Swaziland (Emasisweni) when she moved to South Africa. She left her herd with a family, who in return for taking care of them, owned the calves born of those cows and enjoyed the benefits of milking the cows until the rightful owners came and reclaimed what was theirs. My grandmother was advanced in age and could not travel. She asked my father many times to go and collect her cows, but her efforts were in vain. At last it was time for my brother, her favourite grandson, to pay *lobola* for his beautiful bride. My brother decided to reclaim the cows himself. Within a few days of traveling to Swaziland he was the rightful owner of the cows and was able to pay *lobola* to his bride's parents.

This book is an attempt to restore what the rightful owners have abandoned: our beautiful traditional names. I call on the owners to reclaim them; your names are awaiting you. *Azibuye ezakwethu, azibuye emasisweni.*

But traditional names are not just black names for black people. Many South Africans of all backgrounds have been given African names, though some do not know the meaning of their names. These names have significance to both the name-giver and the one being named. They are containers of memories and significant relationships between parents and children, grandparents and grandchildren, extended families, neighbours and friends, workers and employers, and political and historical personalities and ordinary people. One of my aunts, for example, was a domestic worker who gave each of the children in her care beautiful names. Years after the children had grown up they answered to those names when they visited her. Their names carried rich memories of their childhoods, the time they had spent in the loving care of my aunt. The publisher of this book, Colleen Higgs, grew up in Lesotho and her traditional name is Pulani (daughter of the rain, Sotho). She has named her publishing company Modjaji, after the Balobedu Rain Queen. Because rain is life itself in Africa, there are many versions of the name Rain.

In this book you will find over five thousand South African first names, their origin, and their literal and contextual meaning, as well as notes on traditional South African naming culture. I believe that reclaiming our African names will bring us closer to one another as a nation.

Writing this book

My names are Phumzile Innocentia Simelane-Kalumba.

Innocentia is my school name; my maiden name is Simelane; and my marital name is Kalumba.

I am the last-born in my family and the only girl. Phumzile, which means 'one who has made me rest', is a popular name found in all Nguni languages (siSwati, siNdebele, isiXhosa and isiZulu). My mother named me Phumzile. She so desired a baby girl that she would often go window-shopping and dream of how she would dress her daughter were she ever to be blessed with one. My father, on the other hand, did not want a daughter, whom he feared might disgrace his family by giving birth out of wedlock. My eldest brother was born after my father had been hospitalised with TB for eight months. My father named him Philangenkosi ('am well because of the Lord'). The next child was also a boy and my father named him Bongani ('give thanks'). Then I was born, and my mother's heart rested.

I was born in Piet Retief Hospital in what used to be called the Eastern Transvaal, now renamed Mpumalanga. I attended secondary school in KwaNongoma in Kwazulu Natal and completed a Bachelor of Commerce degree at the University of Cape Town in 1998. In 2000 I married my Ugandan husband, Denis Kalumba. We have three children. I have lived and worked in Johannesburg, Kampala and the United Kingdom. I live in Cape Town now. My travels have helped me to appreciate the languages and traditions we are blessed with in South Africa.

Giving birth to my children was the beginning of this book. My husband wanted our children to have South African names because they are names with meaning. Uganda is a land that has been scarred by many wars. The current naming culture is founded on a religious divide, and most people carry names that primarily indicate whether they are Christian or Muslim. He asked me to write down a few names I liked, together with the meaning of each name, for him to choose from. I began to generate a list of South African names. I started with the names of my family and friends; then I went on to names remembered from my old neighbourhood and from church. Siswati and isiZulu names were easy, since I was born and raised in a home that used these languages interchangeably. SiNdebele names are similar to isiZulu names. IsiXhosa names were more challenging for me because of the Khoe influence on isiXhosa.

Our first born, Sindisiwe (saved; redeemed), was born in Kampala. My husband's huge family and many friends and colleagues surrounded us. He had to explain the meaning of his daughter's name to many people. This was so fascinating to Ugandans that our story ended up in the newspaper – 'Love on foreign soil'. Sindisiwe's hard-to-pronounce name was accepted without question, and with excitement.

In 2001 we went to live in England, where my husband was pursuing his doctorate. Two of our children were born there: Sthembiso ('promise'; the name was given to him by my father) and Kethiwe ('the chosen one'; because God chose to add her to our family). For all the years we were there, there was a wonderful tolerance of and interest in our foreign names, and people always politely asked how to pronounce them correctly, although Sindisiwe became Sindi – sometimes wrongly spelled as Cindy – and Kethiwe became Kethi (sometimes spelled as Cathy).

South Africa's languages

South Africa's constitution guarantees equal status to 11 official languages. These are: Afrikaans, English, isiNdebelele, isiXhosa, isiZulu, Sepedi, Sesotho, Setswana, siSwati, Tshivenda, and Xitsonga. Other languages spoken in South Africa and mentioned in the Constitution are the Khoi, Nama and San languages, sign language, Arabic, German, Greek, Gujarati, Hebrew, Hindi, Portuguese, Sanskrit, Tamil, Telegu and Urdu. This book gives names from nine of our official languages.

Our languages were originally geographically based, and to some extent they still are. In South Africa, the languages you will hear most frequently spoken depend on where in the country you are. IsiXhosa, for instance, is spoken by more than 80% of South Africans in the Eastern Cape, while almost 80% of people in KwaZulu-Natal speak isiZulu. IsiZulu is also the most frequently spoken home language in

Gauteng, but only by a small margin: many other languages are spoken in Gauteng. In Cape Town and its surrounding rural areas, you will often hear Afrikaans spoken, and in the Free State most people speak Afrikaans as a lingua franca. English is the language of business, politics and the media. But it only ranks joint fifth out of 11 as a home language. South Africa's linguistic diversity means all 11 languages have had a profound effect on each other; many South Africans are multilingual, switching with ease from one language to another.

IsiNdebele, isiXhosa, isiZulu and siSwati are often described as 'Nguni' languages, having a common origin in the distant past and many similarities in syntax and grammar. IsiZulu is the mother tongue of 23.8% of South Africa's population, followed by isiXhosa (17.6%). SiSwati is mother tongue to 2.7% of the population, while isiNdebele is mother tongue to 1.6% of the population. The Sotho languages – Setswana, Sepedi and Sesotho – also have much in common. Sesotho is the mother tongue of 7.9% of South Africans; Sepedi is the mother tongue of 9.4% of South Africans, and 8.2% of South Africans claim Setswana as mother tongue. Tshivenda is generally regarded as a language isolate, closer to Shona, a language spoken in Zimbabwe. Tshivenda shares features with Shona and Sepedi, with some influence from the Nguni languages. Tshivenda is mother tongue to 2.3% of the South African population. Xitsonga is home language to 4.4% of the population. Xitsonga is similar to Xishangana, spoken in southern Mozambique, but with some Nguni influences.[1]

Some notes on traditional naming practices

The names in my family carry great meaning. My father has three names, which my grandmother used to speak of her fate when her family forced her to marry my grandfather. When her first husband died she was given in marriage to her deceased husband's brother in accordance with siSwati custom. The first of my father's names is Muzikawungcwatshwa, meaning, 'you do not bury a home'. In other words, when my grandfather's brother was buried, his home was maintained by the remarriage of his widow, as was proper. His second name is Muzikawulahlwa; 'you cannot throw away a home'. In other words, my grandmother felt it was not right to throw away her marriage. His third name is Muzikawaliwa: 'you cannot refuse a home'. She could not refuse the

---

1. These figures are taken from the 2001 Census.

arrangement though she did not want to marry her husband's brother. The name she called my father depended on her mood.

The naming tradition in South Africa was deeply bound up with the stages of life, each of which might be marked by the assumption of a new name: birth, initiation, marriage, the birth of children, and the circumstances of bereavement.

Birth

Traditionally, for the newly wed, the birth of a child was a great blessing; children would be given birth names such as Sandile (we have increased) or Busisiwe (blessed). Giving birth signified that the marriage was a success. Failure to conceive was very painful, especially for the woman; customary dowry, *lobola,* was paid by the husband's family, in exchange for the transfer of fertility, precious children, to the husband's name and family. When a woman gave birth, the child might be named Zibuyile (they have returned) to show that she and her family had fulfilled the bargain; the new mother's status now rose within the marital home and society in general. She might now receive a new name, or be addressed by the name of her child, 'MakaSandile': the mother of Sandile. In South Africa, childlessness was so unacceptable that the husband's family would put their son under great pressure to find another wife who might bring children to the family. In an already polygamous home, a barren wife was subjected to scorn and ridicule by her co-wives. Such names as Boiphemelo (freed from peril), Avhahumi (don't leave me alone), Viwe (God has heard) and Batlile (wanted, have been looked-for) are indications of the tensions within families.

In traditional patrilineal societies, inheritance (name, wealth) is passed down from father to male children. A female child married 'out': she was seen as belonging, ultimately, to another, unknown family, the family of her future marriage. The traditional proverb *ukuwa kwendlu wukuvuka kwenye* (the falling of one house is the flourishing of another) expresses this patrilineal marriage pattern and explains the old male preference for male children, particularly the preference that the firstborn be male, and why certain names (Mfanimpela — it's truly a boy, and Ntombifuthi — it's a girl again) expressed joy or disappointment at the child's sex. Boys brought wives and children (valuable labour power) home; girls gave children to other homes. Of course, even within patrilineal households, mothers often preferred to give birth to daughters, for the help and companionship they offered in the daily round of domestic and agricultural tasks.

Initiation

In the old days, a child was not recognised as fully human, as a person, until he or she had passed through an initiatory event as an adolescent or youth when a new, adult name might be given to mark this important transition. The Christian missionaries adapted these traditional beliefs in the sacrament of baptism, where a new name, often taken from the Bible, was conferred on the convert.

Historical events

In the past, the naming process helped to record important public events that occurred during the time of pregnancy and birth. Children who were born during a destructive invasion of locusts, for example, might be named Tsie (locust), or Sehlolo (disaster). Children born during political unrest might be named Dlame (war, struggle). In the absence of formal birth records, a name could thus be used to estimate the age of its bearer. Although names are no longer used in this way, children may still be named to mark an important event or a critical period in history. Nkululeko (freedom) was a popular name during the liberation of South Africa, and was also given to children born after the first democratic election.

The dark side

In many traditional cultures the evil eye was feared, and naming was one strategy to protect a precious child. Giving a child a name denoting ugliness or other undesired qualities was thought to help avert the evil eye. Although in Sotho tradition to give a child a bad name was to invite bad luck, a family who had suffered infant deaths might give a newborn an unattractive name in order to disguise the child from the Angel of Death.

Some of the names we present here refer to tensions within family and community. A barren woman dares others to speak behind her back when, at last, she gives birth; a polygamous wife celebrates her 'victory' over other wives when she gives birth to more children than they do; a quarrel is remembered; a wife complains about her in-laws, or reproaches a husband who is not pleased at the birth of a child.

The birth of twins brought either great joy or great sadness, depending on the beliefs of a particular group, but special names were always reserved for twins.

Names that signal proverbs

Tshivenda is rich in proverbs. Some Tshivenda names rely on knowledge of these proverbs. For example, Nyadzawela (trouble) signals the proverb *Nya Dzawela*

Vhanwe na sea matshelo zwi do ni welavho, which means, mock someone in trouble and you will be the next to suffer.

Names and gender

While certain nouns that indicate sex have become names, such as *indoda* (man) and *intombi* (girl), which have become the names Ndoda and Ntombi, most names are not exclusively male or female. The meaning and sound of the name is more likely to determine whether the name is given to a boy or a girl. For example, Palesa (flower) is a common girls' name, while Bangizwe (the one fighting for land or born during a civil war) is more likely to be given to a boy. IsiXhosa-speaking boys may be called Phumzile, but amongst isiZulu and siSwati- speakers, Phumzile is a girl's name.

In the Nguni languages neutral nouns such as *inhlanhla* (luck) and *umusa* (grace, mercy) take an extra feminising morpheme, *No* or *Ma*, to become the feminine names Nonhlanhla and Nomusa. The suffix -*kazi* added to a name also indicates sex; Sipho (gift) becomes Siphokazi for a girl. In the Sotho languages, the prefix *Ra* denotes fatherhood; Rapitso is the father of Pitso (the called one). In Tshivenda, the prefixes *Nya-* and *Nwa-* denote the feminine.

Surnames as first names

The use of surnames as first names is an ancient practice. One reason for giving a child such a name was to reinforce the identity of the child and to honour the father and the family to which the child belonged. In some traditions, when a woman got married and changed her surname to her husband's surname, she took her own family name as a first name, and would be addressed by this name in her marital home. This practice ensured that a woman did not entirely lose her original identity as the daughter of her own family, and was also meant to show respect to her as a married woman. However, for females, the feminine form of the family name would be used. Prefixes such as *No-* or *Na-*, which mean 'mother of' and 'daughter of' would be added, for example, Nomathembu, Namnguni. When a male was given a surname as his first name, the name was used without any prefix: Mthembu, Mnguni.

How the names in the book have been presented

Names are presented alphabetically. The meaning of each name follows. The language group of origin is given, in brackets. IsiNdebele, isiXhosa, isiZulu and siSwati names are all designated by (Nguni). Setswana, Sepedi and Sesotho names are designated by (Sotho), while Tshivenda and Xitsonga, language isolates, are indicated by (Tshivenda) and (Xitsonga). While we have great respect for distinct naming traditions, within each language there are many local dialects. IsiXhosa alone has 12 distinct dialects. Naming is the beginning of breaking down walls.

A simple guide to pronouncing vowels:
- a, as in f*a*ther (this sound occurs with many variations in the African languages)
- e, as in p*e*n
- i, as in p*i*ck
- o, as in c*o*rn
- u, as in b*oo*k.

Abbreviations:
- *(f)* – a name usually associated with females
- *(m)* – a name usually associated with males

Abakhe They (the children) are his. *A name given in response to an accusation about a child's paternity.* (NGUNI)

Abonga From the word 'bonga': to give thanks. (NGUNI)

Abongile They (the family) have thanked. (NGUNI)

Aboniwe They (the family) have been seen or attended to. *Children are believed to be a gift from God. In this case, God has seen their need of a child and attended to them.* (NGUNI)

Afika Afikile They (the child) have come. (NGUNI)

Agelalana Live together in peace. *The birth of a child is a chance for a fresh start.* (SOTHO)

Ahlola Judge; decide; condemn. (SOTHO)

Ahlula (m) Defeats the others. *Used in a polygamous family when a woman has given birth to more children than her co-wives.* (NGUNI)

Akanani Akani Akhani (m) You must build. *The parents look forward to the firstborn son's economic contribution to the home.* (XITSONGA)

Akantse A thought. (SOTHO)

Akaziwe (f) She must be introduced. *The child's mother was formally introduced to her in-laws when she was pregnant.* (NGUNI)

Akhekile (m) The family has been built up/increased. (NGUNI)

Akhona Akona (f) Girls are here. *Name given to a child where there are already girls in the family.* (NGUNI)

Alakhe (m) He must build our home. *The parents look forward to the firstborn son's economic contribution to the home.* (NGUNI)

Alidzulwi One cannot stay in this place. *Referring to a situation where people are not allowed to occupy certain land.* (TSHIVENDA)

Alugumi Alu That which does not come to an end. *Usually referring to a fight or quarrel.* (TSHIVENDA)

Aluwa Increase. *The family has increased by the addition of the child.* (VENDA)

Aluwani Grow up; prosper. (TSHIVENDA)

Alwande The children must increase. *Taken from the expression 'usapho alwande': children must increase.* (NGUNI)

Amahle (f) The child is beautiful. (NGUNI)

Amazweni Faraway lands. *Name may be given when the father leaves home to work as a migrant labourer.* (NGUNI)

Ambani Speak up. *The name-giver is using the opportunity to dare those who were gossiping behind her back, saying she is barren.* (TSHIVENDA)

A-mi-na-ndava (f) **Amina** (f) It does not matter to you. *The wife who is ill-treated by her in-laws may communicate a message through this name to her husband, who seems to ignore the fact that she is mistreated by his family.* (XITSONGA)

A-mi-ndzi-lavi (f) **Amindzi** (f) You do not want me. *Name given by a wife who feels hated by her in-laws.* (XITSONGA)

A-mi-swi-lavi (f) **Amiswi** (f) You do not want it. *The father might have expressed feelings of displeasure on hearing the news of the pregnancy.* (XITSONGA)

Amogelang Receive; accept. *The name-giver believes that the child is a gift that has been given to them.* (SOTHO)

Amogetse Received. *See 'Amogelang'.* (SOTHO)

Amohela Receive. *See 'Amogelang'.* (SOTHO)

Amohelang To receive. *See 'Amogelang'.* (SOTHO)

Amose (m) Saviour. *Sotho name of biblical origin, derived from Amos.* (SOTHO)

Amukelani Amukela Amu Accept. *This name will be an encouragement to accept the child as is.* (TSONGA) (NGUNI)

Amuketana Relieve one another in doing something. *This name enforces the ideology that 'it takes the whole village to raise the child'. The name-giver may be too old or unhealthy to raise the child alone.* (XITSONGA)

Anathi They are with us. *The name is a blessing pronouncement. Originally 'they' referred to ancestors, but now the meaning has expanded depending on the belief of the name giver.* (NGUNI)

Anda Increase. *This name is a blessing pronouncement.* (NGUNI)

Andesa Be very many. *This name is a blessing pronouncement.* (TSHIVENDA)

Andile (m) We have increased. (NGUNI)

Andisa Andiswa (f) Cause an increase. *This name is a blessing pronouncement.* (NGUNI)

Andisiwe (f) The family has been increased. (NGUNI)

Andza Grow in number. *This name is a blessing pronouncement.* (XITSONGA)

Anele Aneleyo (f) They are enough. *Usually given to the last-born or when the family has only girls and desires a boy.* (NGUNI)

Anelisa (f) You must satisfy. (NGUNI)

Anelisiwe (f) They have been satisfied. (NGUNI)

Aneliswa (f) Be satisfied. (NGUNI)

Angama Angamela Be in an elevated position and govern. *This name is a blessing pronouncement.* (TSONGA) (NGUNI)

Angarha Embrace. (XITSONGA)

Anokwanda (f) See *'Ayanda'.*

Anwa Increase. *This name is a blessing pronouncement.* (TSHIVENDA)

Apfeswaho The one who listens the most. *The name is to give thanks to God for having listened to the name-giver's prayer.* (TSHIVENDA)

Aphula Free oneself from the moral burden. *The burden in question might be the pressure put on a bride to give birth by her husband or his family.* (XITSONGA)

Apiwe They (the family) have been given [the child]. (NGUNI)

Apreli One born in April. (NGUNI)

Arabang Reply; respond. *The name-giver is thanking God for answering a prayer.* (SOTHO)

Arehone One who is there. *This name refers to the presence of God.* (TSHIVENDA)

Arhosi One born in August. (NGUNI)

Asaduma They (the family) are still becoming famous. (NGUNI)

Asakha They (the family) are still building. (NGUNI)

Asakhe Let us build. (NGUNI)

Asamahle Asemahle (f) She is still beautiful. (NGUNI)

Asamkele (f) Let us accept. *This name may be given when the family expects a boy and receives a girl instead.* (NGUNI)

Asanda (f) We are still increasing. (NGUNI)

Asavela (f) They are still budding or being born. (NGUNI)

Aseza (m) They are still coming. *The name can be given if a girl child was expected. It is a consolation that next time it will be a girl.* (NGUNI)

Asivhanga It is not mine. *Name given when the father disputes that the child is his.* (TSHIVENDA)

Ata Multiply; increase. *This name is a blessing pronouncement.* (SOTHO)

Atama Atamisa Be broad; enlarge. *This name is a blessing pronouncement.* (TSHIVENDA)

Athiambiwi (m) Someone who should not be talked about; someone who must be shown reverence. *Usually someone of authority i.e. chief or headman.* (TSHIVENDA)

Athifhelimbilu I do not get worried. *The name-giver has the opportunity to respond to what is being done to her; usually ill treatment in her marital home or society.* (TSHIVENDA)

Athikhathali One not bothered; does not worry. (TSHIVENDA)

Athilivhali I do not forget. *The name is a warning to offenders not to repeat previous ill-advised actions.* (TSHIVENDA)

Athimangali Not amazed. *The birth of the child is not a surprise.* (TSHIVENDA)

Athinandavha I do not care. *The name-giver is using the opportunity to respond to something that is being done to her, usually ill-treatment.* (TSHIVENDA)

Athini Atini What are they saying now? *The mother might ask this question after having been accused of being barren.* (NGUNI)

Athivhalitshi I will not leave you. (TSHIVENDA)

Athizwilondi I do not care. *Through this name, the name-giver tells the community and family that he/she does not care about all the bad treatment they have received.* (TSHIVENDA)

Athufhedza I have not yet finished. (TSHIVENDA)

Atlarela To receive gladly with open hands. (SOTHO)

Atlega The prosperous one. (SOTHO)

Ausi (f) Sister. (SOTHO)

Avhaathu They have not. *Name depicting poverty in the family.* (TSHIVENDA)

Avhadali Someone who cannot be satisfied. *It is a metaphor for death. Death is personified as someone who greedily asks for more food, where food is equaled to people who are dying.* (TSHIVENDA)

Avhahumi They don't leave me alone. *The name-giver is communicating with those who keep interfering in her affairs, usually the in-laws.* (TSHIVENDA)

Avhapfani They are not getting along. *Names such as this can reveal much about discord in the family.* (TSHIVENDA)

Avhapfeledzi They are not satisfied. *In this case the mother was referring to the in-laws who seemed to feel she was not good enough.* (TSHIVENDA)

Avhasei They are not delighted. *This name warns that there will be adversaries who will not rejoice at the news of the birth.* (TSHIVENDA)

Avhashoni They have no shame. *The name-giver is warning those who have behaved in an ill-advised manner to be ashamed of their deeds.* (TSHIVENDA)

Avhatendi They (the enemies) do not believe. *When someone who has been thought to be barren gives birth, she can give such a name to communicate with those who did not wish her well.* (TSHIVENDA)

Avhavhudzani They don't speak to each other. *This name reveals the situation in the homestead or community.* (TSHIVENDA)

Avhurengwi (m) This position cannot be bought. *Name for royals; one must be born into royalty to occupy certain positions.* (TSHIVENDA)

Aviwe They (the family) have been heard. *Usually after a long period of childlessness.* (NGUNI)

Avukile They have risen. *The child may resemble a dead relative.* (NGUNI)

Awakhe (m) They are his; you must build. (NGUNI)

Awakiwe (m) Let us build. (NGUNI)

Awami (f) Belongs to me. *Name expresses the pride of the name-giver to have her own children.* (NGUNI)

Awande Let the family increase. (NGUNI)

Awela Relax; rest. (SOTHO)

Awelani Awe Rest. (TSHIVENDA)

Awethu The child is ours. (NGUNI)

Ayabonga They (the family) are thankful. (NGUNI)

Ayabulela The family is thankful. (NGUNI)

Ayandza Ayanda They (the family) are increasing. (NGUNI)

Ayibongwinkosi Ayibongwe May He (God) be thanked. (NGUNI)

Azile (f) They (additional members of the family) have come. (NGUNI)

Aziswa (f) To be introduced. (NGUNI)

Azize (f) Let them (bridal cows) come. *When the family of the father has not finished paying lobola.* (NGUNI)

Azola They (the family) are humbled. (NGUNI)

Azwianewi (m) Something that cannot be told. *Usually because of it being shameful; perhaps the child is illegitimate.* (TSHIVENDA)

Azwidali (m) Something that cannot be satisfied; such as death. *Death is related to not having enough children. This name might be given to a child after successive infant deaths.* (TSHIVENDA)

Azwidowi (m) It is not to be repeated. *This name is a warning to those who have previously committed an offense or ill-treatment against the name-giver.* (TSHIVENDA)

Azwifaneli (m) Being under no compulsion. *This may be a response to an ongoing dialogue within a family. The name-giver uses child naming to make her stand.* (TSHIVENDA)

Azwihangwisi (m) Unforgettable. *Here the name-giver is referring to actions done to them; these can be both good and bad. The name serves as a memory of these actions.* (TSHIVENDA)

Azwimmbavhi (m) I am not bothered. *This name is a response to what is being done to the name-giver; usually ill treatment.* (TSHIVENDA)

Azwinaki (m) Something that brings shame to the family. *This name, with its negative connotations, is given in order to protect the child against the evil eye.* (TSHIVENDA)

Azwinndini Azwindini (m) It does not bother me. *This name is a response to what is being done to the name-giver; usually ill treatment.* (TSHIVENDA)

Azwinnyandi (m) Something that does not bring luck to someone. *Name given with the belief that it will protect the child against the evil eye.* (TSHIVENDA)

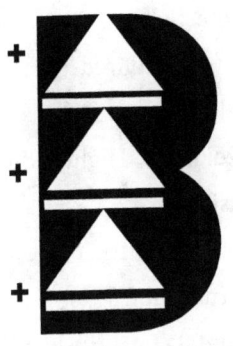

Babalela Take care of the family. (SOTHO)

Babalelang (f) Keep secure. *Child bearing may be viewed as a way of keeping the marriage secure* (SOTHO)

Babalelwa (f) Protected. (SOTHO)

Babalwa Babalo (f) Favoured. (NGUNI)

Babatsa (f) Be celebrated. (SOTHO)

Babazeka Babazekile (f) Highly admired. (NGUNI)

Babazela (f) Praising. (NGUNI)

Babazile (f) Exclaimed! (NGUNI)

Babekati (f) Paternal aunt. (NGUNI)

Babemkhulu Babetala (m) Husband's father. (NGUNI)

Babezala (m) My father-in-law. (NGUNI)

Babhekile (f) They are still waiting for it. *The in-laws have not yet received their gifts from the bride (umabo).* (NGUNI)

Babili (f) They are two. *This name can be used for twins.* (NGUNI)

Baboledi (f) The temperate and calm one. (SOTHO)

Baboloki The one who saves. (SOTHO)

Babongile They (the family) have appreciated [the new addition]. (NGUNI)

Babotegi Trustworthy person. (SOTHO)

Babotlana The younger child. (SOTHO)

Babotse (f) Beautiful person. (SOTHO)

Babusi (m) Of the royal family. (NGUNI)

Badanile (f) They have been disappointed. *Name given to communicate to those who wished the parents an unhappy and childless marriage.* (NGUNI)

Badikazi (f) From 'Dikazi'. Dikazi is an unmarried woman who has a child. (NGUNI)

Badzeli (f) They had given up. *Name given to a child after the parents had given up on having a child.* (NGUNI)

Badzhi (m) Jacket. *Name given to the local tailor.* (TSHIVENDA)

Bafana Boys Boys. *Nickname for the South African soccer team.* (NGUNI)

Bafana (m) Boys. (NGUNI)

Bafedile They have concluded. *This name is an announcement that the family has had enough children* (SOTHO)

Bagcine Take care of the child. (NGUNI)

Bahle (f) The child is beautiful. (NGUNI)

Bahlezi (f) The child is sitting. (NGUNI)

Baholo (m) Elders. (SOTHO)

Bajabhile (f) They are disappointed. *This refers to those who were not wishing the parents well.* (NGUNI)

Bajongeni (m) Look at them. *This expression is said of someone who is shame-faced because something they did not anticipate has happened – in this case the successful birth of the child.* (NGUNI)

Baka (m) Opportunity. (SOTHO)

Bakhangele (m) Behold them. *This name may be a prayer for God to look after the children* (NGUNI)

Bakhetsile (m) They have chosen. *Among the Nguni a young man could have several young girls from which to pick a wife, such a name can be a statement to let the others know that the pick has been made.* (NGUNI)

Bakhile (m) They (the family) have built. *Within Nguni tradition, children are considered vital in the building of the homestead as they continue the husband's lineage to the next generation.* (NGUNI)

Bakhulule (m) Liberate them. *This could be a politically-inspired name.* (NGUNI)

Bako (m) A cave. *Name of the birth place.* (TSHIVENDA)

Balanaganani (m) Scatter. *Such a name could be given if a child was born when the people were being scattered because of a war.* (TSHIVENDA)

Balaseleyo (m) Excellent. (NGUNI)

Baleha (m) Run away. *This may be given as advice to the mother to run away from her in-laws when the paternity of the child is questionable.* (SOTHO)

Baleka (m) Run away. *See 'Baleha' above.* (NGUNI)

Balekisa One causing the other to flee. *The name-bearer might have been born when there was war.* (NGUNI)

Balelisa Outshine others with his/her brilliant beauty. (NGUNI)

Balibele They have forgotten. *The word 'libala' has two meanings; one being 'to forget', the other being 'to be foolish'. Such ambiguity of meaning was sought after when a mother was sending a message to another member of the family.* (NGUNI)

Balincwadi Write a letter. *There was probably a personal situation around the naming of this child that required the writing of a letter.* (NGUNI)

Balindile (f) They have waited. *When a child is born after a long time of waiting.* (NGUNI)

Baliwe Baliswa (f) Has been counted in; must be registered. *The name-bearer was born on the census night.* (NGUNI)

Balulekile (m) Important; distinguished; honourable. (NGUNI)

Balumkile The clever one. (NGUNI)

Balungile They (the family) are good. (NGUNI)

Bambanani Unite. (NGUNI)

Bambhekile They are looking up to him. *Name given to one who is to be a role model; usually the first born.* (NGUNI)

Bambokazi (f) Of the 'Mbambo' family. (NGUNI)

Bandile (m) The family has increased in number. (NGUNI)

Bandla (m)   Congregation. (NGUNI)

Bandzile (m)   The family has increased. (NGUNI)

Bane (m)   There are four children. (NGUNI)

Banele (f)   They (the children) are now sufficient. (NGUNI)

Banesisa (f)   The child is merciful. (NGUNI)

Banetyala (m)   They have committed an offense. *This name is suitable in the case of underage pregnancy, or when the mother was raped.* (NGUNI)

Bangani (f)   What are you quarrelling about? *The child was born when there were quarrels within the family.* (NGUNI)

Bangihlebile (f)   They have gossiped about me. *Child naming may be a chance for the mother to alert the in-laws that she is aware of what they are saying behind her back.* (NGUNI)

Bangiswani (m)   What are they fighting with him for? *The name was given when there was a fight between the father and his brother over the inheritance.* (NGUNI)

Bangizwe   Bangi (m)   Fighting for land. *Can also refer to being born during a civil war.* (NGUNI)

Baningi   They (the children) are many. (NGUNI)

Banobubele   They (the family) are kind-hearted. (NGUNI)

Banomusa   They (the family) have grace. (NGUNI)

Banothando They (the family) have love. (NGUNI)

Banothile They (the family) are wealthy. (NGUNI)

Banoxolo They (the family) have forgiveness. (NGUNI)

Banqobile They have conquered. *This name is derived from a personal experience, something the name-bearer has overcome.* (NGUNI)

Bantu (m) People. *One who is loved by the people.* (NGUNI)

Banyenti (m) They (the children) are many. (NGUNI)

Banzi (m) Wide one; enlarged. (NGUNI)

Baphathe (m) Take care of them (the child). (NGUNI)

Baphelile They (the children) are finished. *When a family has decided not to have any more children.* (NGUNI)

Baphethumusa They (the child) are bearing grace. (NGUNI)

Baphethuthando They (the child) are bearing love. (NGUNI)

Baphethuxolo The child brings reconciliation. *The family believes that the birth will bring peace in the family or between the in-laws.* (NGUNI)

Baphindile They have done it again. *This refers to the mother giving birth again. It can also be given if the mother gives birth to a girl again.* (NGUNI)

Baphiwe The child has been given. *This name is in accord with the belief that children are a gift from God.* (NGUNI)

Baratiwa Beloved one. (SOTHO)

Barulaganye One (child) has come immediately after the other. (SOTHO)

Barwetsana (f) My little daughter. (SOTHO)

Basaledi Remainder. *The family might have experienced infant deaths. Such a name may be given to the surviving child.* (SOTHO)

Basanda The family is still increasing. (NGUNI)

Basani Kindle the fire. (NGUNI)

Basela (f) A small gift. *This name is in accord with the belief that children are a gift from God.* (TSHIVENDA)

Basetsana (f) My little girl. (SOTHO)

Basize (m) You (the child) must help them (the family). (NGUNI)

Batabile (f) One who causes rejoicing. (NGUNI)

Batande Bathande You must love them (the child). (NGUNI)

Batandwa The loved one. (NGUNI)

Batfobile (f) They (the family) are meek. *See 'Thobile'.* (NGUNI)

Bathabile (f) They (the family) are happy. (NGUNI)

Bathandekile (f) She (the child) is lovely. (NGUNI)

Bathandiwe (f) She (the child) is loved. (NGUNI)

Bathandwa (f) Beloved. (NGUNI)

Bathangibaboni (f) They think I do not see them. *The name-giver is using this name to inform offenders that she is aware of what they are doing.* (NGUNI)

Bathathu (f) They (the children) are three. (NGUNI)

Bathembile (f) They (the family) are hopeful. (NGUNI)

Bathethelele (f) Forgive them. *The name is advice to the mother to forgive those who have mocked or ridiculed her, possibly when it was thought she could not get pregnant.* (NGUNI)

Bathini (f) What do they say? *Such a name may be directed to those who had talked about the mother being barren.* (NGUNI)

Batho People. (SOTHO)

Bathobekile Bathobile (f) The humbled one. (NGUNI)

Bathokozile (f) They (the family) are happy. (NGUNI)

Batjele (f) Tell them (gossipers) that the birth was successful. (NGUNI)

Batlile (f) The child has been wanted; looked for. (SOTHO)

Batusile (f) They (the family) have admired. (NGUNI)

Bavumile (f) They have agreed. *When the father has accepted the pregnancy as being his doing.* (NGUNI)

Bawelile (f) They (the parents) have crossed over. *Such a name may be given to a first-born to commemorate the parents moving to the next level of parenthood.* (NGUNI)

Bawinile (f) They are victorious. *When a child is what has been desired by the parents/family.* (NGUNI)

Baxolile (f) They have forgiven. *Sometimes the birth of a child can bring reconciliation to family feuds.* (NGUNI)

Bazamile (f) They have tried. *This name refers to the birth of a child after trying several times to have a baby.* (NGUNI)

Bazini (f) What do they know? *Question-type name, revealing confusion in the family.* (NGUNI)

Bazothini (f) What are they going to say? *Question-type name, revealing confusion in the family.* (NGUNI)

Bazuzile (f) They (the family) have gained. (NGUNI)

Bebenya (f) Glitter; shine. (SOTHO)

Bekezela (f) Endure hardship. (NGUNI)

Bekitemba (m) Hoping in someone. *The name-bearer is regarded as the hope for the name-giver.* (NGUNI)

Belinda (f) They (the family) have waited. (NGUNI)

Benele (f) They (the children) are enough. (NGUNI)

Bereng (m) Name of a former Sotho chief. (SOTHO)

Besabakhe (m) The son of his. *Name given when the family has more boys than girls.* (NGUNI)

Besana (m) Boys. (NGUNI)

Bezile They (the child) have come. (NGUNI)

Bhadazela (m) Walk cautiously in or on. *Traditional folktale name. Bhadazela was a clumsy looking character but a faithful and truthful servant; he performed acts of bravery and was generously rewarded by the King.* (NGUNI)

Bhambatha Comforts; gently pats on the back. (NGUNI)

Bhambathiso Promise. (NGUNI)

Bhambatisa Cheer by promise. (NGUNI)

Bheka (m) Look; watch; take care of. *Also a short form of 'Bhekabantu'.* (NGUNI)

Bhekabantu (m) Look after the people. *A combination of 'bheka' and 'bantu'.* (NGUNI)

Bhekamuphi (m) Who is responsible? *Usually for the misfortunes that were surrounding the birth.* (NGUNI)

Bhekaphezulu (m) The one looking up to God. (NGUNI)

Bhekathina (m) Look to us. *A combination of 'bheka' and 'thina'.* (NGUNI)

Bhekinhlanhla (m) One who looks out for opportunities. *A combination of 'Bheka' and 'Nhlanhla'.* (NGUNI)

Bheki Bhekinkosi (m) Look to the King (God). *A combination of 'Bheka' and 'Nkosi'.* (NGUNI)

Bhekisisa (m) Watch carefully; be cautious. (NGUNI)

Bhekithemba (m) The hope we are looking to. (NGUNI)

Bhekizifundiswa (m) Watch (and learn from) the educated ones. *A combination of 'Bheka' and 'Izifundiswa'.* (NGUNI)

Bhekizitha (m) Watch out for the enemies. (NGUNI)

Bhekizizwe (m) One to rule the nations. (NGUNI)

Bhekokwakhe (m) One who watches over his own possessions. (NGUNI)

Bhekukwenza (m) Look at their deeds. *Each society has persons highly admired for their acts; such a name will be given to encourage the bearer to grow up emulating such characters.* (NGUNI)

Bhekumuzi (m) Look after the household or descendants. *A combination of 'Bheka' and 'Umuzi'.* (NGUNI)

Bhekuzalo (m) Watch over the clan. (NGUNI)

Bhelekazi (f) Daughter of the Bhele family. (NGUNI)

Bhidisa (m) One who causes the other to err. *Such a name may be given to a child born from a teenage pregnancy.* (NGUNI)

Bhinqela (m) Strive for. (NGUNI)

Bhungu (m) Young and sturdy man. (NGUNI)

Bhunguka (m) Been away from home for a long time. *Especially when a father went to work in the mines and has not been back for a long time.* (NGUNI)

Bihamiri (m) Ugly one. *The name-giver is venting her anger/sadness over being ill-treated and wonders whether the mistreatment is due to her ugliness.* (XITSONGA)

Bikwa (f) Reported one. *This name is given to a teenage pregnancy and according to custom the family of the girl must 'bika' (report) to the family of the boy in order that his family pay a fine.* (NGUNI)

Bikwaphi (f) Where should we report her? *This name reflects that the mother did not know who the father of her child was. According to the Nguni custom the child is reported in the father's home.* (NGUNI)

Bindzile Bindza (f) The quiet one; be quiet. (NGUNI)

Bizekile (f) Be renowned. (NGUNI)

Bizo (m) Name. *People with the same name can use this name to refer to one another.* (NGUNI)

Boa (m) Come back; return. (SOTHO)

Bobono (m) Handsomeness; beauty. (SOTHO)

Bobotse Beauty. (SOTHO)

Bogega Worthy to be looked at; beautiful. (SOTHO)

Bohlale Wisdom. (SOTHO)

Bohlokoa (f) Precious one. (SOTHO)

Bohlokwa (m) One who commands respect and is of significance. (SOTHO)

Bohlokwahlokwa (m) Scarce; precious; rare. (SOTHO)

Boiketlo (m) Lavishness; extravagance. (SOTHO)

Boikhutso (m)   Rest; holiday. (SOTHO)

Boipeletso   One with appeal. (SOTHO)

Boipelo   Gladness of soul. (SOTHO)

Boiphediso   Of good health; success. (SOTHO)

Boiphemelo   Freed from peril. *Sometimes such a name can be given after difficulty in giving birth.* (SOTHO)

Boitaolo (m)   The self-willed boy. (SOTHO)

Boithabiso (m)   Causing rejoicing. (SOTHO)

Boithibo (m)   Self-controlled and guided. (SOTHO)

Boitlotlo (m)   Self-regard. (SOTHO)

Boitsebo (m)   Self-awareness. (SOTHO)

Boitsheko (m)   Purity. (SOTHO)

Boitshepo (m)   Trusting. *Parents may have prayed, trusting that God would give them this child.* (SOTHO)

Boitswarelo (m)   Forgiveness. *The birth of the child can bring reconciliation to family feuds.* (SOTHO)

Boitswaro (m)   Behaviour and attitude. (SOTHO)

Boitumelo (f)   One bringing joy and delight. (SOTHO)

Bokang   Praise; rejoice. (SOTHO)

Bokgwabo   Kind-hearted one. (SOTHO)

Bokhutso   Place of rest. (SOTHO)

Bolekane   Companionship. (SOTHO)

Boleng   Existence. (SOTHO)

Boleta   To love and to cherish. (SOTHO)

Bomanyano   They (the family) are united. (NGUNI)

Bomi Life. (NGUNI)

Bomikazi (f) Great life. (NGUNI)

Bomvana The little red one. (NGUNI)

Bonakala Come out of hiding. (NGUNI)

Bonakele (f) Has been seen. (NGUNI)

Bonang (f) Look! *Exclaiming at the birth of a baby girl.* (SOTHO)

Bonani You must perceive. *Through this name the bearer is drawing the attention of the relevant party to a particular situation that may be going on within the home.* (NGUNI)

Bonatla (m) Courageous. *Courage is a desirable male quality in many societies.* (SOTHO)

Bonelela Treat the child with care. (NGUNI)

Bonga Bongani (m) Give thanks. (NGUNI)

Bonganjalo The family is ever grateful. (NGUNI)

Bongeka (f) One who is praiseworthy. (NGUNI)

Bongekile (f) We are thankful. (NGUNI)

Bongelwa (f) We are celebrating the birth. (NGUNI)

Bongephiwe (f) Give thanks for the gift. (NGUNI)

Bongile (f) Thanked. (NGUNI)

Bonginkosi Give thanks to God. (NGUNI)

Bongi Bongiwe We have thanked. (NGUNI)

Bongoe Oneness; unity. (SOTHO)

Boni Bonisisa (f) Clearly understand. (NGUNI)

Bonisiwe (f) Been advised. (NGUNI)

Boniwe (f) Has been seen. (NGUNI)

Bonke (m) All of them. *When it is a house with sons only.* (NGUNI)

Bonnete Truth. (SOTHO)

Bono Short form of 'Bonokwakhe'. (NGUNI)

Bonokuhle One who sees good only. (NGUNI)

Bonokwakhe One who sees to his own. (NGUNI)

Bonolo Ease; meekness. (SOTHO)

Bontle Brilliant beauty. (SOTHO)

Bootee Unity; oneness. (SOTHO)

Bopelonolo Meekness; tenderness. (SOTHO)

Bopelotelele Patience; endurance. *See also: 'Mamelelo'.* (SOTHO)

Bophelo Life itself. (SOTHO)

Bopile Has moulded. (SOTHO)

Bopilwe (f) Has been created. (SOTHO)

Boratehi (f) Charming one. (SOTHO)

Boratelo (f) Home of love. (SOTHO)

Bosali (f) With feminine qualities. (SOTHO)

Boteng Presence. *The name-giver is expressing thanks to the Lord for confirming His presence in their lives through the gift of a child.* (SOTHO)

Botle (f) The beautiful one. (SOTHO)

Botlhale (m) Man with wisdom. (SOTHO)

Botona (m) Highly ranked. (SOTHO)

Botse (f) Beautiful; graceful. (SOTHO)

Botsebotse (f) Very beautiful/graceful. (SOTHO)

Botshelo Life. (SOTHO)

Boya Bowa Return. (SOTHO)

Buang Speak. *The name-giver is using the opportunity to dare those who were gossiping behind her back.* (SOTHO)

Bubele The kind one. (NGUNI)

Buhlalu (f) One adorned with beads. *Traditionally, beads were the only attire for some Nguni girls.* (NGUNI)

Buhlaluse (f) One with many beads. Traditional folktale name. *Buhlaluse was a beautiful princess in Zulu folklore, always adorned with many beads which made her maids jealous to such an extent that they plotted her murder and buried her alive. However, she was rescued by her prince charming.* (NGUNI)

Buhle (f) Brilliant beauty. (NGUNI)

Buhlebemvelo (f) Natural beauty. (NGUNI)

Bukekile (f) One worthy to behold. (NGUNI)

Bukelile (f) One watching from the side. (NGUNI)

Bukelwa (f) One to be admired. (NGUNI)

Bukhosi (f) Royalty or princehood. (NGUNI)

Bukiwe (f) The fair one to be looked at. (NGUNI)

Books Royalty. (XITSONGA)

Bulela Give thanks. (NGUNI)

Bulelani Be grateful. (NGUNI)

Bulelwa (f) Thanked. (NGUNI)

Bulumko (m) Wisdom. (NGUNI)

Bulundlela (m) Road opener; one who makes the way. (XITSONGA)

Bunono (m) The well organised one. (NGUNI)

Buntfu (m) Human nature. (NGUNI)

Buntu (m) One with humanity. (NGUNI)

Busa (m) Reign; govern. (SOTHO)

Busago (m) One who is reigning/governing. (SOTHO)

Busani (m) You must reign. *Name for royalty.* (NGUNI)

Buselaphi Busaphi (f) Where is the domain to govern? (NGUNI)

Busisa (f) Blessed. (NGUNI)

Busisiwe Busi (f) The blessed one. (NGUNI)

Busiswa (f) God's favoured one. (NGUNI)

Busiwe (f) With one reigning over her. (NGUNI)

Butho (m) An army. (NGUNI)

Butholezwe (m) The young, well-born warrior of his land. (NGUNI)

Buto (m) A bundle of joy. (TSHIVENDA)

Buyani Return. *Sometimes the birth coincides with the death of a family member and the birth will be considered a return of the deceased member.* (NGUNI)

Buyelekhaya Return home. *A call to those in exile.* (NGUNI)

Buyelwa Have returned. (NGUNI)
Buyiselwa Being returned. (NGUNI)
Buyiswa Buyisiwe Buyi Brought back. (NGUNI)
Buzile Have asked. (NGUNI)
Buzwe Of the land. (NGUNI)

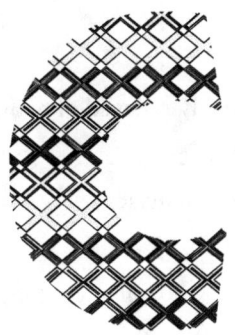

Cabangile (f) Well thought of. (NGUNI)

Cabumuzi (f) The one who will decorate the home. (NGUNI)

Cacile (f) Perfectly clear. *The child's resemblance makes it clear who the father is.* (NGUNI)

Calawa (f) Be quickly relieved of pain. (XITSONGA)

Candzata Enrich. (XITSONGA)

Cebazinto One who advises. (NGUNI)

Cebile   Cebi (f) Rich. (NGUNI)

Cebisa (f) The one who enhances the lives of others. (NGUNI)

Cebisayo (f) *See 'Cebazinto'.*

Cebisile   Cebisiwe (f) To enrich; to advise. (NGUNI)

Cebo (m) Planned for. (NGUNI)

Cebolakhe   Cebolenkosi (m) His (God's) plan. (NGUNI)

Cebolihle (m) Good plan. (NGUNI)

Cebolikayise (m) According to her father's plan. *Sometimes the man will come from the mines with the intention to impregnate the wife during the holiday.* (NGUNI)

Celamandla (m) Ask for strength. (NGUNI)

Celani (m) Ask. *The child has been asked for from God.* (NGUNI)

Celekuphila (m) Asking for long life. (NGUNI)

Celenhle (f) Asking for a beautiful child. (NGUNI)

Celesile (f) We have rejoiced. (NGUNI)

Celimpilo Celi (f) Seeking healthy life. (NGUNI)

Celinhlanhla (f) Ask for luck and good fortune. (NGUNI)

Celisiwe (f) Requesting on behalf of. (NGUNI)

Celiwe (f) The one whom we have asked for. (NGUNI)

Celo Celokuhle (m) Asking that the child gets what is good. (NGUNI)

Celokwakhe (m) Asking for her own. *In this name, the name-giver is indirectly addressing a message to her debtor; it may be that the husband has not finished paying the lobola.* (NGUNI)

Celumusa Asking for grace. (NGUNI)

Cemula Suddenly become enriched. (XITSONGA)

Chamukile Chamkile The child has appeared. (NGUNI)

Chansenga (f) A girl entering puberty. (XITSONGA)

Chavana (m) Show respect for one another. (XITSONGA)

Chavani (m) The chief. (XITSONGA)

Chavelela (m) Console yourself. *That is, after the death or loss of something treasured, console yourself with this child.* (XITSONGA)

Chimbula (m) Abundant supply. *The child might have been born almost at the same time as the other children within the home.* (XITSONGA)

Chithumuzi (m) One who destroys the home. *In this case, one of the relations was being accused of destroying the home through the use witchcraft.* (NGUNI)

Chokisela (f) Do well. (NGUNI)

Chokisile (f) She (the mother) has done well. (NGUNI)

Chuma (f) Be fruitful. *It is a blessing declared upon the child.* (NGUNI)

Chumani (f) Bud/flourish. *It is a blessing declared upon the child.* (NGUNI)

Chumela (f) Flourish. *It is a blessing declared upon the child.* (NGUNI)

Chumile (f) Has budded. (NGUNI)

Chwayita (f) Be happy. *It is a blessing declared upon the child.* (NGUNI)

Chwayitisile (f) One who has made us joyful. (NGUNI)

Ciko (f) One who pays attention to details. (NGUNI)

Cingile (f) Has been thought about. *The mother might have hoped for a child of a particular sex.* (NGUNI)

Cocisiwe (f) One who is free from blemishes. (NGUNI)

Colani (m) You must forgive. *This name is a plea for reconciliation in conflict-laden situations.* (NGUNI)

Combelile (f) She (the mother) has done her best. (NGUNI)

Cwaka (f) Quietness. (NGUNI)

Cwebezela (f) Sparkle with beauty. (NGUNI)

Cwebile (f) Clear; be pure as water. (NGUNI)

Dakalo Daki (m) One bringing happiness. (TSHIVENDA)

Dakeni (m) Premature baby boy. (XITSONGA)

Dali (m) Satisfy. (TSHIVENDA)

Dalindlela (m) The one who has paved a way. (NGUNI)

Dalumzi (m) The home-maker. (NGUNI)

Daluvuyo (m) One who causes happiness. (NGUNI)

Daluxolo (m) The peacemaker. *The birth of a child can mean an end to family feuds.* (NGUNI)

Dambanyika (m) This is the name of the first Vha Venda chief of Njelele valley. (TSHIVENDA)

Dambisa (m) The one who soothes away the pain. *This name can be given after the death of a loved one.* (NGUNI)

Dambuza (m) Someone who walks slowly. (NGUNI)

Daniele (m) Judgment of God; God is my judge. *Sotho name of biblical origin, derived from Daniel.* (SOTHO)

Danisa (m) Doing better than others, in a competitive situation. *Such a name may be given in a polygamous home where the wives may be competing against one another.* (TSONGA) (NGUNI)

Danisani (m) Make sad. (NGUNI)

Danisile (f) You have made us sad/disappointed us. (NGUNI)

Delani (m) You must give up. *The name-giver is using this name to communicate to rivals or those who were not wishing her a successful relationship.* (NGUNI)

Delile (f) One who just had enough. *The name-giver may use this name to communicate her grievances in spite of power relations at play.* (NGUNI)

Delisa (f) Satisfy. (NGUNI)

Delisile Delisiwe (f) One who has been satisfied. (NGUNI)

Deliwe (f) The rejected one. *In this case, the father decided to end the relationship on finding out that the mother was pregnant.* (NGUNI)

Demana (m) **Demazane** (f) Traditional folktale name. *These were two siblings who mischievously let loose the fortune bird from its cage. Running away from the punishment of her parents, Demazane throws herself into the sea. Instead of drowning, she is crowned a sea goddess by the king of the waters.* (NGUNI)

Dembe (m) Miracle. *The birth of a baby to a childless couple can be regarded as a miracle.* (TSHIVENDA)

Denga (m) Punished. *Could have been derived from the following Tshivenda proverb: 'Tshe wa lilela musanda wo tshi wana, ṇungu ya denga yo no vha mukuloni': one who was causing trouble in the area, is now arrested or punished because of his/her deeds.* (TSHIVENDA)

Diboko (m) Praises. (SOTHO)

Dibote (f) Beautiful. (SOTHO)

Dideka Confused. *Such a name can be use to indirectly communicate feelings about a certain situation within the home.* (NGUNI)

Didi It (the child) is precious. (NGUNI)

Digela Praise. (SOTHO)

Dihlahlang In the bush. *May refer to where the child was born.* (SOTHO)

Dihlohlong Being put to shame. *This may refer to an illegitimate child or a child born from a teen pregnancy.* (SOTHO)

Dikazi (f) An unmarried woman who has given birth to a child. (NGUNI)

Dikeledi (f) Tears. (SOTHO)

Dimakatso (f) Surprises; amazements. (SOTHO)

Dimbanyika (m) One who refused land given to him. (TSHIVENDA)

Dimo (m) A man-eater in Basotho legends. (SOTHO)

Dimpho Gifts; presents. (SOTHO)

Dina (f) Burdensome. *Sometimes the birth of a child may be perceived as an extra load to a mother who is already suffering in her marital home.* (NGUNI)

Dinda (m) Messenger of the chief. (XITSONGA)

Dinekedza (f) Surrender. (TSHIVENDA)

Dineo (f) Grants; gifts; talents. (SOTHO)

Dinette (f) Truth. (SOTHO)

Dinga (m) Promise. (NGUNI)

Dingane (m) The needed one. (NGUNI)

Dingani (m) What are we in need of? *Zulu chief overthrown by the Boers in 1840.* (NGUNI)

Dingindawo (m) One looking for shelter. *Sometimes a child is born during a certain need in the family, such as a need for shelter.* (NGUNI)

Dingiswayo (m) Banishment. *First name of King Shaka Zulu's mentor (1780–1817).* (NGUNI)

Dingwayo (m) The one who is needed. (NGUNI)

Dintle (f) Beauty. (SOTHO)

Dintletse (f) Abundance. (SOTHO)

Dipalesa (f) Flowers. (SOTHO)

Dipuo (f) The one who carries gossip around. (SOTHO)

Disebo Whispers. (SOTHO)

Disego (f) Laughter. (SOTHO)

Disemba (f) One born in December. (NGUNI)

Ditebogo (f) Thanks. *This name is in accord with the belief that children are a gift from God, for which one should be thankful.* (SOTHO)

Dithwele (f) Dust found in the house. *Given after successive infant deaths to protect the child against an evil eye.* (SOTHO)

Ditiro (f) Acts. (SOTHO)

Ditshego Ditsheho (f) Laughter. (SOTHO)

Ditswalo (f) Motherly grace and mercy. (XITSONGA)

Ditswanelo (f) Suitable things. (SOTHO)

Ditumo (f) Desires; wishes. (SOTHO)

Dlame (m) Struggle. *One born during an uprising.* (NGUNI)

Dlani (m) What are we to eat? *When the child was born the family was struggling for survival; the grandmother's pension being the only source of provision.* (NGUNI)

Dojiwe (f) One who has been picked. *This is a protective name.* (NGUNI)

Donsekhaya (m) Bring us home. *Such a name may be related to the 'Buyisa' custom performed among Nguni ancestral worshippers. It is a ritual done with the hope that the dead ancestors will come back and watch over the living.* (NGUNI)

Dovhani (m) Repeat. *This name obtains its meaning from its social context; it may be the repeat of female/male children, e.g. good done to her.* (TSHIVENDA)

Dowelani Dowe (m) Get used to it. *Name-giver is expressing her emotion about a certain situation in the family.* (TSHIVENDA)

Duduza Dudu Duduzani Duduzile Comfort. (NGUNI)

Dumani (m) Famous son. (NGUNI)

Dumazile (f) One who has disappointed. (NGUNI)

Dumezweni Famous throughout the land. (NGUNI)

Dumile Famous one. (NGUNI)
Dumisani Dumi Dumisile Give praises. (NGUNI)
Dumisiwe (f) He (God) is praised. (NGUNI)
Dumiso Praise. (NGUNI)
Dyahatani (m) Careless person. (XITSONGA)
Dyondza (m) Learn. (XITSONGA)
Dyondzisa (m) Teach. (XITSONGA)
Dzanani (m) A place of quarrels. (TSHIVENDA)
Dzanga (m) Battle axe. (XITSONGA)
Dzanga (f) Beautiful. (TSHIVENDA)
Dzangakuwa (m) Eldest son. (XITSONGA)
Dzangalelo (m) Interest. (XITSONGA)
Dzata (m) Peace; refuge. (TSHIVENDA)
Dzinga (m) Keep on doing. (XITSONGA)
Dzingandleve (m) One who turns a deaf ear. (XITSONGA)
Dzivamisoko April. *Name can be given to a child born in April.* (XITSONGA)
Dzivula Sudden increase. (XITSONGA)
Dzovo The skin. (XITSONGA)
Dzubhana Not yet complete. *Usually given for a small and premature baby.* (NGUNI)
Dzudzanyani (m) Put things in order. *Requesting the new arrival to sort out things in the homestead.* (TSHIVENDA)
Dzula Dzulani Stay; sit. (TSHIVENDA)
Dzumuka Become prosperous after poverty. (XITSONGA)

Dzunani Must praise. (XITSONGA)
Dzuneka Be praiseworthy. (XITSONGA)
Dzunisa Dzuni Dzunisani Praise. (XITSONGA)

Edisa Cause to radiate. (SOTHO)
Edzani Be liked. (TSHIVENDA)
Elami Short for 'Gugulami'. (NGUNI)
Elelwani (f) Remember. (TSHIVENDA)
Elethu (f) Short for 'Gugulethu'. (NGUNI)
Elihle (f) Beautiful and bright future. (NGUNI)
Eliqhakazile (f) Brighter; fair; beautiful rose. (NGUNI)
Emela (f) Stand by; support; wait for. (SOTHO)
Emihle (f) The beautiful one. (NGUNI)
Enamile (f) Joyful. (NGUNI)
Eniša Enrich cause to prosper. (SOTHO)
Entlani The child must do what is expected of him/her. (XITSONGA)
Entle (f) The beautiful one. (NGUNI)
Enye Another one. (NGUNI)
Esabo (m) The one belonging to them. (NGUNI)
Esaia (m) The salvation of the Lord. *Sotho name of biblical origin, derived from Isaiah.* (SOTHO)
Esakhe (f) The one belonging to her/him. (NGUNI)
Esihle (f) The beautiful one. (NGUNI)
Esomusa (f) Of grace. (NGUNI)
Estere (f) Secret; hidden. *Sotho name of biblical origin, derived from Esther.* (SOTHO)
Ezekiele (m) The strength of God. *Sotho name of biblical origin, derived from Ezekiel.* (SOTHO)

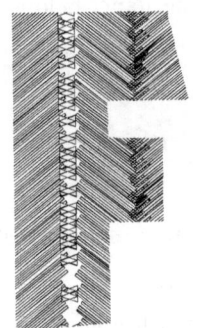

Fakazile (f) One who has witnessed. *Probably regarding the validity of the relationship between the mother and the father.* (XITSONGA)

Falakhe (m) The inheritance belongs to him. *Name usually given to the first-born son.* (NGUNI)

Fambisa (m) Guide. (XITSONGA)

Fanele Fanelwe Worthy one. (NGUNI)

Fanelwa That which suits you well. (NGUNI)

Faniswa One resembling someone else. (NGUNI)

Fano Fanozi (m) Boy. (NGUNI)

Fana Fanyana (m) Little boy. (NGUNI)

Faranani (m) Work together. *This name carries a message of cooperation.* (TSHIVENDA)

Felleng (m) Beyond the end. (SOTHO)

Fezeka (f) Accomplishment. (NGUNI)

Fezekile (f) Has been accomplished. (NGUNI)

Fezile (f) Has fulfilled the promise. (NGUNI)

Fezisa (f) Helps to complete. (NGUNI)

Feziwe (f) Ambition achieved. (NGUNI)

Fezokuhle The one who will accomplish what is good. (NGUNI)

Fezwa Done. (NGUNI)

Fhatuwani Fhatu Be careful; be alert. (TSHIVENDA)

Fhedzisani Fhedzi Finish. (TSHIVENDA)

Fhulufhedzani Fhulu Be hopeful. (TSHIVENDA)

Fhulufhelo (f) Hope. (TSHIVENDA)

Fhulufhuwani (m) Forget it! *Protective name.* (TSHIVENDA)

Fihlakele (f) Hidden one. (NGUNI)

Fihlama Fihlamani Be hidden; be concealed. (XITSONGA)

Fikanaye Has come with the child. *In this case, the grandmother gave this name to imply that the daughter-in-law came to her marital home pregnant with another man's child.* (NGUNI)

Fikelephi (f) What kind of place has she arrived at? *The name reveals that there was no proper home suitable for to the birth of a baby.* (NGUNI)

Fikile Fiki Has arrived (i.e. is born). (NGUNI)

Fikiswa (f) One who has been welcomed in a new place. (NGUNI)

Fikitlikili (m) Short, sturdy person. (XITSONGA)

Filemone (m) One who kisses. *Sotho name of biblical origin, derived from Philemon.* (SOTHO)

Filwego The gifted one. (SOTHO)

Fiselega Yearning for. (SOTHO)

Fisiwe The one who has been so desired. (NGUNI)

Fisokuhle Fiso The one who desires good. (NGUNI)

Fuduka Pack up and go. *In this case, the farm owner had expelled the parents when the mother was pregnant.* (NGUNI)

Fulufhelo Hope. (TSHIVENDA)

Fuma Rule. (XITSONGA)

Fumane Found; discovered. (SOTHO)

Fumani Be rich. (XITSONGA)

Fumisa Put in authority. (XITSONGA)

Funa To love. (TSHIVENDA)

Funanani Love one another. (TSHIVENDA)

Funani What are you searching for? *This name may be given to a father who is still involved in extra-marital affairs instead of settling down with his wife.* (NGUNI)

Fundile Has learnt the lesson. *Name may be given to the mother by the grandmother in the case of teenage pregnancy* (NGUNI)

Fundisiwe Fundi Fundiswa Able to learn from others. (NGUNI)

Fundzisile Educated one. (NGUNI)

Funẹa Loveable. (TSHIVENDA)

Funeaho Amiable. (TSHIVENDA)

Funeka The one who has been searched for. (NGUNI)

Funokukhulu Funo (m) Wanting a big share. *Name given when there was an inheritance dispute in the family around the birth of the child.* (NGUNI)

Funokwakhe (m) One who wants his own. *In this case, the father was bitter with his relatives who took his inheritance whilst he was very young. This is a chance to claim what is his through the name of his child.* (NGUNI)

Fura Be satiated. (TSHIVENDA)

Fusha Satisfy. (TSHIVENDA)

Fushea Be satisfied. (TSHIVENDA)

Futhi Again. *Name given when the parents have another boy/girl.* (NGUNI)

Fuyata (m) Breach birth. (XITSONGA)

Fuyateya (f) Girl who was born with legs first. (XITSONGA)

Fuzile Bearing resemblance. (NGUNI)

Fuzunina (f) Resembling the mother. (NGUNI)

Fuzuyise (m) Resembling the father. (NGUNI)

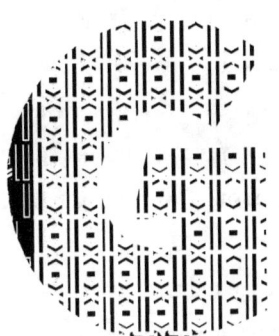

Gaba (f) Garnish; beautify. (NGUNI)

Gabile (f) Adorned. (NGUNI)

Gabisile (f) We are proud of her. (NGUNI)

Gabonolo (m) Soothingly. (SOTHO)

Gada (m) Watch out. *This name is a warning or threat uttered by the name-giver that her enemy should anticipate serious consequences for their actions.* (NGUNI)

Gagu A bold person. *This name is also given to someone who likes singing.* (NGUNI)

Galamba (m) Huge man. (XITSONGA)

Gamalakhe Her/His name. (NGUNI)

Gamelihle (f) Beautiful name. (NGUNI)

Ganephi (f) Where is your marital home? *In this case, the mother-in-law was not happy that her daughter-in-law constantly left to visit her own parents.* (NGUNI)

Gangata To make a point. (NGUNI)

Ganyetela One bearing false witness to a family dispute. (XITSONGA)

Gaobonale God is hidden. (SOTHO)

Gaone (m) Of Him (God). (SOTHO)

Gatsha (m) A branch. (NGUNI)

Gava (m) Sow again where the first seed has failed to grow. (XITSONGA)

Gavela Tying around the body. *The waistcloth women wear when they carry a child on their back, is symbolic of closeness between the mother and child.* (XITSONGA)

Gazi (m) Blood. *Usually referring to a blood relation.* (NGUNI)

Gcalagcala (m) Fierceness; hot temper. (NGUNI)

Gcebekile Gcebile (f) Have made things right. (NGUNI)

Gcina (f) To keep safe. (NGUNI)

Gcinakele (f) She has been kept safe. (NGUNI)

Gcinaphi (f) Where are you going to end? (NGUNI)

Gcinikhaya Gcinimzi (f) Take care of the home. (NGUNI)

Gciniwe (f) Well kept. (NGUNI)

Gcobani (m) To be anointed; to be happy. (NGUNI)

Gcobisile Gcobisa Cause happiness. (NGUNI)

Gcotyelwa One we are happy about. (NGUNI)

Gcotyiswa (f) Made to rejoice. (NGUNI)

Gcwizi Just missed. *This name could be used to mock a rival who was also eyeing the same woman for marriage.* (NGUNI)

Gedleyihlekisa (m) Beat or hurt while laughing. *The complete sentence is 'Ngeke ngithule umuntu engigedla engihlekisa' meaning: I won't be quiet if someone is pretending to be my friend whilst causing me harm. This is an example of a dispute name.* (NGUNI)

Gegerhemba (m) Obstinate man. (XITSONGA)

Gezani Cleansing. *Name also used in Tsonga folktales.* (TSONGA) (NGUNI)

Gezile She has washed. (NGUNI)

Ginqitshe (m) The one who rolls away the stone or removes a stumbling block. *The birth of a child can be a huge breakthrough for the mother in her relationship with her in-laws or husband.* (NGUNI)

Gobotse (f) Beautiful; fine; suitable. (SOTHO)

Godiraone (m) It is Him (God) who acts or who does. (SOTHO)

Godisa (m) Cause to grow; bring up; rear. (SOTHO)

Gofaone (m) It is Him (God) who gives. (SOTHO)

Gofejana (m) The youngest child in the family. (SOTHO)

Gofenyang (m) Who has defeated. *In this case, the father went to World War II when the mother was pregnant.* (SOTHO)

Gogo (f) Grandmother. (NGUNI)

Goitsemang Who knows? (SOTHO)

Goitseone Goitsemodimo It is Him (God) who knows. (SOTHO)

Gomela Return. (SOTHO)

Gomisa Cause to return; bring back. (SOTHO)

Gomodo (m) One with a big forehead. (XITSONGA)

Gongomela Evening star. (XITSONGA)

Goniwe (f) The cuddled one. (NGUNI)

Gosego (m) Lucky is he. (SOTHO)

Gosiame (m) One born under fine conditions. (SOTHO)

Gota (m) Headman. (TSHIVENDA)

Gqibeliso (m) Giving birth for the last time. *Name given when the family decides it has enough children.* (NGUNI)

Gqumela (m) Concealed. (NGUNI)

Gugile The aged one or wise one. *A child born to mature parents.* (NGUNI)

Gugulami My treasure. (NGUNI)

Gugu Gugulethu Our precious one. (NGUNI)

Gumani (m) Stop. *Name bestowed after a dispute over a boundary; telling the offenders not to do it again.* (TSHIVENDA)

Gumba (m) Take everything. (XITSONGA)

Gundo (m) Victory. *Name reflecting the event leading to victory.* (TSHIVENDA)

Guqa (m) Kneel. (NGUNI)

Guqulisizwe (m) The one who changes the nation. (NGUNI)

Gwatshaza (m) One who is shy or afraid. (NGUNI)

Hahla (m) **Hahlakazi** (f) Fraternal twins. (XITSONGA)

Hakamela (m) On the balance. *A stick one throws at a tree is said to 'hakamela' when it remains on the branch and does not fall back. Name given to the only boy among girls.* (XITSONGA)

Hakelo (m) Reward. (XITSONGA)

Hakundwi (m) Cannot be defeated. *Derived from the expression 'Mudzimu u a kundiwa' meaning: God cannot be defeated.* (TSHIVENDA)

Halaletsa (m) Be holy. (SOTHO)

Hambanyisa (m) Disunite. (XITSONGA)

Hambile One who has gone. *The father returned to the mines when the child was born.* (NGUNI)

Hambukela Make way for someone. (XITSONGA)

Hambukisa Lead astray. (XITSONGA)

Hamolemo Gently. (SOTHO)

Hanedza Refuse to admit. (TSHIVENDA)

Hangwa (m) Forget. (TSHIVENDA)

Hangwani Hangwi (m) Forget. *See also 'Azwihangwisi'.* (TSHIVENDA)

Hangwela (m) Forgiveness. (TSHIVENDA)

Hanyani Let them (the child) live. (XITSONGA)

Hanyeleni What is the good of living? *The mother experienced a misfortune so great that even the child's birth could not comfort her.* (XITSONGA)

Hanyisa Make alive. (XITSONGA)

Hawe (m) His. *The child belongs to God.* (TSHIVENDA)

Helelani Complete. *That is, the family is complete.* (XITSONGA)

Heleleta Do something for the last time. *Meaning that this is the last child to be born.* (XITSONGA)

Hetisani Complete. *That is, the family is complete.* (XITSONGA)

Hetiseka To accomplish. (XITSONGA)

Hitekani Prudence. (XITSONGA)

Hlabelani Let there be singing. (NGUNI)

Hlahlelihlelokubiyela (f) A beautiful, fortifying bough. (NGUNI)

Hlakanipha Be wise. (NGUNI)

Hlakanyana (m) Traditional folktale name. *Hlakanyana was a trickster in a Nguni folktale.* (NGUNI)

Hlalanathi Stay with us. (NGUNI)

Hlalaphi (f) Where would she stay? *The name reveals the lack of shelter or poor housing conditions that the family may have been facing at the time of birth.* (NGUNI)

Hlalefa Be wise. (SOTHO)

Hlalezwini Stick to the word of promise. *This name may be given as a reminder for one to fulfil their promise* (NGUNI)

Hlaluka Something quite extraordinary. *The child can closely resemble a family member who has died and it can be considered as a return of the deceased.* (XITSONGA)

Hlalusela Explain. (XITSONGA)

Hlamalane Hlamalani Amazement. (XITSONGA)

Hlamarisa Astound; astonish. (XITSONGA)

Hlamatsega (f) Be beautiful. (SOTHO)

Hlambamandla This is the same as 'I am washing my hands', meaning: I deny responsibility for it. *There was probably a personal situation around the naming of this child.* (XITSONGA)

Hlamu Solution to a problem. (XITSONGA)

Hlamukile They have all rejected me. (NGUNI)

Hlamula Answer. (XITSONGA)

Hlamulo Answered prayer. (XITSONGA)

Hlanganani Be united. *The birth of the child should be a uniting point for the family.* (NGUNI)

Hlangananyeta Bring together. (XITSONGA)

Hlanganaswo Whatever you met. *Usually not a good thing.* (XITSONGA)

Hlanganyela Coming together to accomplish a task. (NGUNI)

Hlanganyeti The one who gathers dry wood for the fire for another to kindle it. *That is, 'the one who shows no anger, but stirs up others'.* (XITSONGA)

Hlanzeka Be pure. (NGUNI)

Hlanzekile (f) The pure one. (NGUNI)

Hlawulani Choose. (XITSONGA)

Hlawulekani Be the best amongst many others. (XITSONGA)

Hlayisa Guard. *Prayer to God to guard the family.* (XITSONGA)

Hlayisani Be preserved. (XITSONGA)

Hlayiseka Be saved. (XITSONGA)

Hlebani Go ahead and gossip. (NGUNI)

Hlelile Hle Have planned. (NGUNI)

Hleliwe (f) She has been planned for. (NGUNI)

Hlelo A plan. (NGUNI)

Hlelolwenkosi God's plan. *This name can be given when the birth was unplanned by the parents.* (NGUNI)

Hlelolwethu Our Plan. (NGUNI)

Hlelulane Laugh at her suffering. *An expression of contempt for the adversaries who find the mother's plight amusing; the name-giver downplays the impact of their actions by encouraging them to continue.* (XITSONGA)

Hlengani Rescue. (XITSONGA)

Hlengiwe Hlengi (f) Rescued. *The birth of a child can be a rescue from mockery, especially in a polygamous home.* (NGUNI)

Hleziphi (f) Where are you delayed? *Name can be given for a delayed labour.* (NGUNI)

Hlobile (f) The pure one. (NGUNI)

Hlobisile (f) The adorned one. (NGUNI)

Hlodile Predicted. (SOTHO)

Hlogonolofala Become blessed. (SOTHO)

Hlomekile (f) One who has been easily misled by evil influences. *A name given to a child from a teenage pregnancy.* (NGUNI)

Hlomela Be armed, bold and courageous and ready for life ahead. (NGUNI)

Hlomile The armed one. (NGUNI)

Hlomisa (f) Newly-wedded woman. (XITSONGA)

Hlompho Respect. *This is also the name of a tradition where the name of a respected personality is substituted for another as a sign of esteem.* (SOTHO)

Hlomula To get an award. (NGUNI)

Hlonipha Respect. (NGUNI)

Hloniphile (f) One with respect. (NGUNI)

Hlosukwazi One who yearns to know. (NGUNI)

Hlotswe Has been created. (SOTHO)

Hloyiwe Hated. *In this case, the mother was not accepted and loved by her in-laws.* (NGUNI)

Hlulani Overcome. (NGUNI)

Hluma You must grow. (NGUNI)

Hlumelela To grow again. (NGUNI)

Hlumelelisa Cause to bud/restore. *The mother gave the name as a prayer ; 'Hlumelelisa Umoya wami', meaning: restore my soul.* (NGUNI)

Hlumile Hlumi The budding one. (NGUNI)

Hlupase Making them suffer. (NGUNI)

Hluphekani Suffer. (XITSONGA)

Hluphekile (f) One in distress. (XITSONGA)

Hluphizwe Hluphi He who harasses the nation. (NGUNI)

Hluphuyise Worry your father. (NGUNI)

Hlweka Become clean/clear/good. (SOTHO)

Holofetsa Performance of what has been promised. (SOTHO)

Hologo Salvation. (SOTHO)

Holopang Remembrance. (SOTHO)

Homotsa Console; comfort. (SOTHO)

Hosi (m) Master. (XITSONGA)

Hosona (m) Petty chieftaincy. (XITSONGA)

Hudza (m) Enhance. (TSHIVENDA)

Hulisani Huli (m) Make it big. (TSHIVENDA)

Hulwane (m) Senior. (TSHIVENDA)

Huma (m) Rise. (XITSONGA)

Humbelani Humbe (m) Ask. (TSHIVENDA)

Humbulani Humbu (m) Remember. (TSHIVENDA)

Humelelani (m)   Be successful. (XITSONGA)

Humile (m)   Become rich. (SOTHO)

Ikahlolela (m) Judge (for oneself). (SOTHO)

Ikgethetse Chosen. (SOTHO)

Ikhona (m) He (God) is with us. (NGUNI)

Ikhutse (m) Must rest. (SOTHO)

Ilotse (m) Revived (by medicine); rendered harmless; rescued. (SOTHO)

Inamandla (f) The Lord has power. (NGUNI)

Inami (f) The Lord is with me. (NGUNI)

Inathi (f) The Lord is with us. (NGUNI)

Inathinkosi (f) God is with us. (NGUNI)

Indhuna (m) Headman or the Chief. *This name reflects the position held by the name-giver.* (XITSONGA)

Ingiphile (f) The Lord has given me. *This name is in accord with the belief that children are a gift from God.* (NGUNI)

Inkosazana (f) The princess. (NGUNI)

Inkosi (m) The king. *This is a royal name; also a praise name for the Dlamini clan.* (NGUNI)

Inkulu (m) Eldest son. *This is a birth rank name.* (NGUNI)

Inosizi (f) God has mercy. (NGUNI)

Inothando (f) The Lord has love. (NGUNI)

Iphendule (f) Short form of 'Nkosiphendule'. (NGUNI)

Isiphile (f) Short form of 'Nkosisiphile'. (NGUNI)

Isivile (f) The Lord has heard us. (NGUNI)

Itani (m) Do it. *The child is given this name to dare those behind deaths in the family that they should stop; if they do not stop they will be caught.* (TSHIVENDA)

Ithandile (f) Short form of 'Nkosithandile'. (NGUNI)

Itshepa Be pure. (SOTHO)

Itshwarela Forgiveness. (SOTHO)

Itumeleng (f) Be joyous. (SOTHO)

Ivumile Short form of 'Nkosivumile'. (NGUNI)

Jabhile (f) Disappointed. (NGUNI)

Jabhisile Jabsi Jabsile (f) The one who causes disappointment. *Name usually given when the parents have been expecting a boy and a girl is born instead.* (NGUNI)

Jabulani Jabu (m) You must rejoice. (NGUNI)

Jabulile (f) Rejoicing. (NGUNI)

Jabulisile (f) One who causes rejoicing. (NGUNI)

Jabuliswa (f) One who is delighted. (NGUNI)

Jaha (m) Young man. (XITSONGA)

Jakobo (m) One that supplants/undermines; the heel. *Sotho name of biblical origin, derived from Jacob.* (SOTHO)

Jamela (m) Bold and defiant one. *Female version of Jama. Also a character in Niki Daly children stories.* (NGUNI)

Janabari (m) One born in January. (NGUNI)

Jeremia (m) Exaltation of the Lord. *Sotho name of biblical origin, derived from Jeremiah.* (SOTHO)

Jeso (m) Saviour; deliverer. *Sotho name of biblical origin, derived from Jesus.* (SOTHO)

Jobo (m) He that weeps or cries. *Sotho name of biblical origin, derived from Job.* (SOTHO)

Joele (m) He that wills or commands. *Sotho name of biblical origin, derived from Joel.* (SOTHO)

Johanne (m) The grace or mercy of the Lord. *Sotho name of biblical origin, derived from John.* (SOTHO)

Jokisile (m) The persistent one. (NGUNI)

Jonase (m) A dove; he that oppresses; destroyer. *Sotho name of biblical origin, derived from Jonah.* (SOTHO)

Jongikaya (m) One who will watch over the home. *Responsibility falls on the child to be the economic stabiliser of the home.* (NGUNI)

Jongikhaya (m) Look after the home. *Responsibility falls on the child to be the economic stabiliser of the home.* (NGUNI)

Jongilanga (m) He faces the sun. *Meaning one who has faced lots of difficulty: 'Facing the heat'.* (NGUNI)

Jongile (m) Being looked at. *The bride in an Nguni home is constantly watched and criticised. At the birth of a child, she may use the name to ask for some space.* (NGUNI)

Jongintaba (m) Looking over the mountain. (NGUNI)

Jongisisa (m) Look carefully. (NGUNI)

Jongiwe (m) One who is watched. (NGUNI)

Jongizizwe (m) Looking over the nations. *This name can be given to a royal as it signifies authority.* (NGUNI)

Josefa (m) Increase; addition. *Sotho name of biblical origin, derived from Joseph.* (SOTHO)

Juguja (m) Swing something violently. *Name given to a fighter.* (SOTHO)

Julayi One born in July. (NGUNI)

Juni One born in June. (NGUNI)

Kabelo (m)　Our Portion. (SOTHO)

Kabo (m)　That which has been given. *The gift being the child.* (SOTHO)

Kaela (m)　Guiding. *This name may signify the future role of the child.* (SOTHO)

Kagiso (m)　Friendship; peaceful co-existence. *This name may refer to relationships between members of the family or in the community.* (SOTHO)

KaJama (m)　The son of 'Jama'. (NGUNI)

Kakaramba (m)　Hefty and strong person. *Name based on physical appearance.* (NGUNI)

Kalambu (m)　Keep silent. *This name was the response of the name-giver to a group of people who disapproved of her life-style.* (XITSONGA)

KamaGeba (m)　The son of the Zulu clan. (NGUNI)

Kamnandzi　Pleasantly. *The name may be a narrative about the birth experience of the mother.* (NGUNI)

KamNguni (m)　The son of the Ngunis. (NGUNI)

Kamohelo (m)　Acceptance; welcome. (SOTHO)

Kananelo　Approval; appreciation. (SOTHO)

Kanelo　Enough. (NGUNI)

Kanya　Rich. *A blessing declaration.* (XITSONGA)

Kanyisa　The light-bringer. (NGUNI)

Kanyisile　The one who put the light on. (NGUNI)

Karabelo Karabo An answer. *The parents had been praying for the child for a long time.* (SOTHO)

Kataza Making them suffer. *This name is a puberty name the girl gave to herself. In this message she is addressing the boys who might be sexually interested in her. The name is also a statement of her moral stand and the expression of her expectations from her present or potential suitors.* (NGUNI)

Kateka Be happy. *A blessing declaration.* (XITSONGA)

Katekani Be blessed. *A blessing declaration.* (XITSONGA)

Katekisa Cause happiness; be a blessing. *A blessing declaration.* (XITSONGA)

Katlanego (m) Achievement. (SOTHO)

Katlego Katleho (m) Triumph. (SOTHO)

Kawaliwa (m) Cannot be refused. *The mother was forced into marriage. Such a name can be conceived as the consolation of the powerless, that inward vengeance which we call consolation or solace.* (NGUNI)

Kawulahlwa (m) Cannot be overthrown. *The birth of the child ensures the continuity of the family lineage.* (NGUNI)

Kawungcwatswa (m) Cannot be buried. *Short form of 'Muzikawungcwatswa'.* (NGUNI)

Kaya (m) Home. *Name given within the prevailing African context that one must have children to build a home* (NGUNI)

Kaya mune (m) What is his home? *This is a case of questionable paternity.* (XITSONGA)

Kayalandile (m) The home has increased. *Name given within the prevailing African context that one must have children to build a home.* (NGUNI)

Kayalethu (m) Our home. *Name given within the prevailing African context that one must have children to build a home.* (NGUNI)

Kayise (m) Belonging to the father. *This name is associated with paternity issues.* (NGUNI)

Keabetswe I have been given. *This name is in accord with the belief that children are a gift.* (SOTHO)

Kealeboga I am grateful. *This name is in accord with the belief that children are a gift.* (SOTHO)

Keamogetse I have received. *This name is in accord with the belief that children are a gift.* (SOTHO)

Keamohetswe I have been welcomed. *At the birth of a child among the Sothos, the mother receives a new higher status within the homestead.* (SOTHO)

Keatametse Closer to God. *The name-giver may have been praying to God for a child.* (SOTHO)

Kedibone I have observed. *This name is a self-reflection based on an assessment of the situation in which the name-giver has been ill-treated. She disconnects herself from the situation and in so doing downplays the impact of their actions on her emotions.* (SOTHO)

Kedibonye I have observed. *Same as 'Kedibone'.* (SOTHO)

Kefeletswe I have lost hope. *This name was given to the child by the grandmother when an uncle took to drinking.* (SOTHO)

Kefilwe I have been given. *This name is in accord with the belief that children are a gift.* (SOTHO)

Kegaugetswe I have received compassion and mercy. *Name given after the couple had difficulty conceiving.* (SOTHO)

Keitumetse I am happy; I am thankful. (SOTHO)

Kekeletso Addition. (SOTHO)

Keketso (m) An addition. (SOTHO)

Kelebogile Kelebohile I am grateful. *This name is in accord with the belief that children are a gift.* (SOTHO)

Kelebone I have seen you. (SOTHO)

Kelello Understanding. (SOTHO)

Keletlgoko One who gives careful thought. (SOTHO)

Keletsi Dictated by wisdom. (SOTHO)

Keletso Desire to fulfill an aspiration. (SOTHO)

Kemelo Been waited for. (SOTHO)

Kenako It is time. *From the expression 'Ke nako': meaning it is about time. The expression is used when something is long overdue. The same expression was used when South Africa hosted the 2010 FIFA World Cup.* (SOTHO)

Kenaluena I am with you. (SOTHO)

Keneiloe Keneilwe Keneoue Keneuwe I have been given. *This name is in accord with the belief that children are a gift.* (SOTHO)

Kenosi I am alone. *The child was born when the father had separated from the mother.* (SOTHO)

Keolebile Looking to God. (SOTHO)

Keratile I have loved. (SOTHO)

Keratiloe I have been loved. (SOTHO)

Keromang (m) One who was sent. (SOTHO)

Ketapele (m) Leader. (SOTHO)

Keteko (m) Festivity. *In most cultures, the child is welcomed joyously amidst festivities.* (SOTHO)

Kethiwe (f) The chosen one. (NGUNI)

Ketsahalo (m) Momentous event. (SOTHO)

Ketsiwe (f) *See 'Kethiwe'.*

Ketso One who fulfills an exploit. (SOTHO)

Ketsogile One who is well. (SOTHO)

Kgabo (m) Chimpanzee. *This name, with its negative connotations, is given in order to protect the child against the evil eye.* (SOTHO)

Kgadi (f) The only girl in the midst of boys in the family. (SOTHO)

Kgaetsedi Kgaitsadi (f) Sister. (SOTHO)

Kgakgamatso A suprise. (SOTHO)

Kgalalelo Glory. (SOTHO)

Kgantšha Brighten. (SOTHO)

Kganya Proud. (SOTHO)

Kgarebe (f) Mature maiden. (SOTHO)

Kgathola (m) Experience. (SOTHO)

Kgatlha (m) One who is admired. (SOTHO)

Kgatlhego (m) Pleasure. (SOTHO)

Kgaugelo Kgauhelo (m) Compassion; pity; mercy; grace. (SOTHO)

Kgethang Choose. (SOTHO)

Kgethilwe Kgethwa Was chosen; elected; picked. (SOTHO)

Kgodiso (m) Praise; honour. (SOTHO)

Kgokgo (m) Ugly and unattractive. *Protective name given after successive infant deaths.* (SOTHO)

Kgomotso One who has comforted us. *A child born after a tragedy in a family can bring comfort.* (SOTHO)

Kgopolo Opinion. (SOTHO)

Kgorane Rich one. (SOTHO)

Kgoroto (m) Champion; leader. (SOTHO)

Kgorula The youngest child in the family. (SOTHO)

Kgosi (m) King or royalty. (SOTHO)

Kgosiemang (m) Who is the chief? *Such a name can be given when the chieftaincy is disputed.* (SOTHO)

Kgosietsile (m) The Lord has come. (SOTHO)

Kgothatso (m) One who has comforted us. *The child may have been born after a tragedy in the family.* (SOTHO)

Kgotso (m) Peace; tranquility. *This name carries a message of peace and cooperation.* (SOTHO)

Kgwabo (m) Kind-hearted. (SOTHO)

Kgwahla (m) Become strong/firm. *Blessing declaration.* (SOTHO)

Kgwari (m) Neat one. (SOTHO)

Kgwathile (m) Be strong. (SOTHO)

Khabane (m) Valuable; precious; warrior. (SOTHO)

Khabonina Khabo (f) She belongs to her mother's home. (NGUNI)

Khakhathi (m) Troublesome. *This name may remind the family of problems they experienced when the child was born.* (TSHIVENDA)

Khalanga (m) Direction. *A birth may help the parents to determine the direction that they need to take, such as to settle down in marriage.* (XITSONGA)

Khaliphile (f) Sharp and clever one. (NGUNI)

Khangayo (f) One who is very attractive and has charming beauty. (NGUNI)

Khangekile Khangile (f) Attractive one. (NGUNI)

Khangelani (m) Gaze upon. *This name may reflect amazement at the miraculous birth.* (NGUNI)

Khangezile (f) One with the expectation to receive. (NGUNI)

Khanghela Look up. (XITSONGA)

Khangisela (f) One with enlightenment. (NGUNI)

Khangwe A short form of 'Khangwelo'. (TSHIVENDA)

Khangwelo Forgiveness. (TSHIVENDA)

Khanisa Khanisani Help one another to succeed. (XITSONGA)

Khankha Dance for joy at the event. *In this case it will be the birth of a new child.* (XITSONGA)

Khanuka Be astounded. *This name may reflect amazement at the miraculous birth.* (XITSONGA)

Khanya (f) The illuminating/shining one. (NGUNI)

Khanyakule (f) Shining. (NGUNI)

Khanyakwezwe (f) Light of the world. (NGUNI)

Khanyisa (f) Light up. (NGUNI)

Khanyisela (f) One who brings the light for others. (NGUNI)

Khanyisile Khanyo (f) One who has brought the light. (NGUNI)

Khanyisiwe Khanyi (f) You have been illuminated. (NGUNI)

Khanyiso (m) The light. (NGUNI)

Khathazile (f) Troubled. (NGUNI)

Khathutshelo Khathu Forgiveness. (TSHIVENDA)

Khauhelo Compassion; pity. (SOTHO)

Khawuleza Be swift. *This name may be given when the labour was long and tiresome to the mother.* (NGUNI)

Khaya (m) A home. *Name given within the prevailing African context that one must have children to build a home.* (NGUNI)

Khayakazi (f) Big home. *The birth of a child signifies an increase in the home.* (NGUNI)

Khayalakhe (m) His home. *Name given within the prevailing African context that one must have children to build a home.* (NGUNI)

Khayalami (m) My home. *Name given within the prevailing African context that one must have children to build a home.* (NGUNI)

Khayalenjabulo (m) Home of rejoicing. *This name tells people to be happy after the birth of this child.* (NGUNI)

Khayalentokozo (m) Home of joy. *This name tells people to be happy after the birth of this child.* (NGUNI)

Khayalethu (m) Our home. *Name given within the prevailing African context that one must have children to build a home.* (NGUNI)

Khayalomusa (m) Home of grace. (NGUNI)

Khayaloxolo Home of forgiveness. . *The birth of this child is expected to bring a stronger sense of unity among family members* (NGUNI)

Khayelihle A wonderful home. (NGUNI)

Khayelitsha A new home. *Name given within the prevailing African context that one must have children to build a home.* (NGUNI)

Khazamula Shine. (XITSONGA)

Khazimula Khazimla Shine; glow with beauty. (NGUNI)

Khazimulisa Cause to shine. (NGUNI)

Khensani Khensane Showing gratitude. (XITSONGA)

Khensile Have thanked. (XITSONGA)

Khetha Choose. (NGUNI)

Khethamuphi Which one will you choose? *Such a name will be given when the father has a number of women with whom he is involved.* (NGUNI)

Khethang Choose. (SOTHO)

Khethani What do you choose? (NGUNI)

Khethelihle Choose the best one. (NGUNI)

Khethikhaya Choose the home. (NGUNI)

Khethiwe Khethi (f) Chosen. (NGUNI)

Khethizwe One who has chosen to live a life of worldly pleasures. (NGUNI)

Khethokuhle One who makes good choices. (NGUNI)

Khethukuthula Choosing peace. (NGUNI)

Khethumuzi Choosing to keep the home. (NGUNI)

Khethuxolo Choosing to forgive. (NGUNI)

Khetselo (f) The best among the rest. (NGUNI)

Khetsiwe (f) Chosen. (NGUNI)

Khitsitiwe (f) Of abundance. *Suitable for multiple births.* (NGUNI)

Khokela (f) Lead. (NGUNI)

Khokelela (f) Lead to. (NGUNI)

Khokho Great-grandparent. (NGUNI)

Kholakele Kholeka Kholekile (f) **Koleka** (f) **Kolekile** (f) The trustworthy one. ()

Kholelwa (f) Have faith. (NGUNI)

Kholisa Kholisile (f) She has satisfied. (NGUNI)

Kholiswa (f) Caused to be satisfied. (NGUNI)

Kholiwe (f) The believer. (NGUNI)

Kholiwe (f) Satisfied with what we have. (NGUNI)

Kholofediso (f) Promise. (SOTHO)

Kholofelo (f) Hope. (SOTHO)

Kholokholo (m) Adam's apple. (XITSONGA)

Kholwa Kholwani Believe. (NGUNI)

Kholwangokubona The one who always must see to believe. (NGUNI)

Khoma Care for. (XITSONGA)

Khomale Pardon. (XITSONGA)

Khomanani Caring for each other. (XITSONGA)

Khombisile Khombi (f) She has shown them; one who directs. (NGUNI)

Khombo (f) Misfortune. *Name used after successive infant deaths.* (XITSONGA)

Khombomuni (f) What kind of misfortune? *Name used after successive infant deaths.* (XITSONGA)

Khomotso (f) A consolation. (SOTHO)

Khongotela (f) Comforter. (XITSONGA)

Khonza (f) To admire. (NGUNI)

Khonzeka (f) The one who is well liked. (NGUNI)

Khonzunina (f) She prefers her mother. (NGUNI)

Khonzuyise (m) The one who likes her father much. (NGUNI)

Khosi (m) One of royalty.

Khotavuxika (m) June. *Name can be given to a child born in June.* (XITSONGA)

Khotsimunene (m) Paternal uncle. (TSHIVENDA)

Khotso (m) Peace. (SOTHO)

Khotsofalang (m) Be satisfied. (SOTHO)

Khulani (m) Grow up; increase. *Blessing declaration.* (NGUNI)

Khule (m) Short form of 'Khulekani', 'Khulelaphi'. (NGUNI)

Khuleka   Khulekani (m) Pray. (NGUNI)

Khulekela (m) To regard highly with honour. (NGUNI)

Khulekile (f) Had prayed for the child. *This name might be given when a family has been struggling to have a child or if there were complications with the pregnancy.* (NGUNI)

Khulelaphi (f) Where should she grow up? *Such a name could be employed for a child born to teenagers, who could be raised on either the maternal or paternal side.* (NGUNI)

Khulile (f) She has grown up. (NGUNI)

Khulula Set free. *Giving birth means that the mother can be free of observing certain taboos within the homestead; such a name could be used to commemorate that.* (NGUNI)

Khululiwe The one who has been set free or liberated. *Giving birth means that the mother can be free of observing certain taboos within the homestead; such a name could be used to commemorate that.* (NGUNI)

Khuluma Speak. *Such a name may be a response those who were talking behind the mother's back about her inability to give birth. She is daring them to speak.* (NGUNI)

Khumagadi (f) Woman of great importance. (SOTHO)

Khumbu A short form of 'Nkhumbudzeni' and 'Nkhumbuleni'. (TSHIVENDA)

Khumbuka Remind oneself of past events. (XITSONGA)

Khumbulani You must remember. *One who stands to remind the family of a certain event, probably surrounding the birth.* (NGUNI)

Khumbulile (f) Has been remembered. *This name may be given after a long wait for the child, in order to say 'God has remembered me'.* (NGUNI)

Khumbuzile (f) The one who reminds. *One who stands to remind her family of a certain event, probably surrounding the birth.* (NGUNI)

Khumiso Enhancement. (SOTHO)

Khumo Wealth; riches. (SOTHO)

Khumoetsile Wealth has come. (SOTHO)

Khungelekile (f) Gracious one. (NGUNI)

Khunjulwa (f) One who is being remembered. (NGUNI)

Khunjuzwa The reminder. *One who stands to remind the family of a certain event, probably surrounding the birth.* (NGUNI)

Khupereto Take hold of the hand. (SOTHO)

Khusela One who is well protected. (NGUNI)

Khuselekile Secured. (NGUNI)

Khuselwa Be cuddled. (NGUNI)

Khuthadzo Appeasement. (TSHIVENDA)

Khuthala The hard working/diligent one. (NGUNI)

Khuthazela Continue steadfastly. (NGUNI)

Khuthazile (f) Has been encouraged. (NGUNI)

Khuthele (f) Hard worker. (NGUNI)

Khutla (m) Return. (SOTHO)

Khutsa (m) Rest. (SOTHO)

Khutsago (m) One who rests/reposes. (SOTHO)

Khutsalo (f) Diligent. (NGUNI)

Khutsatile (f) An encouragement. *The birth of a child may be an encouragement to the parents to stay together.* (NGUNI)

Khutse Must rest/repose. (SOTHO)

Khutsitse Calm and peaceful. (SOTHO)

Khutso Quietness and rest. (SOTHO)

Khuzwayo One who needs constant chastening. (NGUNI)

Khwatini In the forest. *Name based on the place where the mother gave birth when she went to gather wood.* (XITSONGA)

Khwela Climb up higher. (NGUNI)

Khwelisa Help one to be lifted. (NGUNI)

Khweti (f) Shining morning star. (NGUNI)

Khweza Elevate; promote. (NGUNI)

Khwezikazi (f) A huge morning star. (NGUNI)

Kilela (f) Take care of yourself. (SOTHO)

Kimollo (m) One who brings relief. (SOTHO)

Kinita (m) The well-built boy. (SOTHO)

Kitlana (m) Become close to one another. (SOTHO)

Kitsego (m) Renown; fame. (SOTHO)

Kitsho (m) The knowledgeable one. (SOTHO)

Kitso (m) Knowledge. (SOTHO)

Kobamelo (m) Act of worshipping. (SOTHO)

Koketso (m) Increase and adding on. (SOTHO)

Kokobela (m) Become humble. (SOTHO)

Kokobetsa (m) Humble. (SOTHO)

Kokobetsi (m) The modest person. (SOTHO)

Kokomana A great-grandchild. (SOTHO)

Kokotlegelo (m) Prosperity. (SOTHO)

Kokotletsa (m) Support. (SOTHO)

Koliswa (f) *See 'Kholiswa'.*

Koliwe (f) Has believed. (NGUNI)

Kologana (m) Follow one another. (SOTHO)

Kolometse (m) The sun has set. (SOTHO)

Kolwane (m) The well-built young man. (SOTHO)

Koma (m) Celebrating victory. *This name can be given after a boy has successfully finished circumcision school.* (SOTHO)

Konanani Kone Be good to one another. (TSHIVENDA)

Kongwane A plant with clusters of yellow flowers. *This name may signify the place of birth.* (SOTHO)

Kontraka (m) Agreement; contract. *Family members are urged to work together through the naming of this child.* (SOTHO)

Kopano Kopana Kopanelo (m) Unity; meeting together; sharing together. *The birth of this child is expected to bring a stronger sense of unity among family members.* (SOTHO)

Kopelo (m) Tune; hymn. (SOTHO)

Kopo (m) Requested. *The parents had prayed for the child.*

Korogela (m) You have come. *Such a name may be given when the child is believed to be a re-birth, i.e. is one of the ancestors who has come back.* (SOTHO)

Kotlhao (m) Punishment. *This name was given to a teenage pregnancy. The girl's getting pregnant was viewed as punishment for having been involved in sexual activities before marriage.* (SOTHO)

Kotulo (m) A harvest. *The child may have been born during the harvest season.* (SOTHO)

Kovo-kovo (m) Eyes deep in their sockets. *This will be a nickname for someone with such features, rather than a given name.* (XITSONGA)

Kowa (m) Be heard. *The name-giver had prayed for a child.* (SOTHO)

Ku feni (m) In death. *A child born when a mother underwent complications which threatened her life.* (XITSONGA)

Kufanelekile The appropriate one. (NGUNI)

Kuhle It is good. (NGUNI)

Kukile Lifted; picked up. (SOTHO)

Kulani (m) Grow. *A blessing declaration.* (XITSONGA)

Kulula Set free. (NGUNI)

Kulungile It is all good. (NGUNI)

Kumbulani Remember. *One who stands to remind her family of a certain event, probably surrounding the birth.* (NGUNI)

Kumnandisi The one who sweetens things. (NGUNI)

Kunabelela Wish. (XITSONGA)

Kunda Defeat. (TSHIVENDA)

Kungeka Be confused. (NGUNI)

Kuphelile It has been accomplished. (NGUNI)

Kurisa Enlarge. (XITSONGA)

Kusasa Tomorrow; the future. *Parents may look at the children as the retirement fund for when they are old.* (NGUNI)

Ku-saseka Goodness. (XITSONGA)

Ku-saseka-i-vanwana Goodness is the goodness of others. *Taken from a proverb meaning 'When you are good then others will also be good'.* (XITSONGA)

Kusaselihle (f) Beautiful future. (NGUNI)

Kusaseliqhakazile (f) Bright future. (NGUNI)

Kuselwa (m) The protected one. (NGUNI)

Kutala (m) Be diligent. (NGUNI)

Kuthula (m) The quietness. (NGUNI)

Kutlo (m) Bound to obedience. (SOTHO)

Kutlwisiso Kutloisiso Kutloano Kutlwana

Kutlwano (m) Mutual understanding/agreement. *The birth of this child is expected to bring a stronger sense of unity among family members* (SOTHO)

Kutsokombela (m) Sweet one. (XITSONGA)

Kuvhanganani Kuvha (m) Gather; come together. *The birth of this child is expected to bring a stronger sense of unity among family members.* (TSHIVENDA)

Kuzwana (m) Harmony. *The birth of this child is expected to bring a stronger sense of unity among family members.* (NGUNI)

Kwaela Watch closely. (SOTHO)

Kwagalo One skilled in logic. (SOTHO)

Kwago Obedient. (SOTHO)

Kwahlula Triumph. (NGUNI)

Kwakhe Belonging to her or him. *This name reflects a change in the general belief that an African child is the child of the community.* (NGUNI)

Kwakhelana Build for one another. (NGUNI)

Kwala Be understood. (SOTHO)

Kwalago That which is heard. (SOTHO)

Kwana (m) Lamb. (SOTHO)

Kwana Small child. (TSHIVENDA)

Kwanatla Strong; energetic. (SOTHO)

Kwandakwethu (f) This is how we have increased. (NGUNI)

Kwandisa (f) Has caused an increase. (NGUNI)

Kwanele (f) We have had enough. *When a family has decided that they have enough children or girls.* (NGUNI)

Kwano (m) Consent. *The birth of this child is expected to bring a stronger sense of unity among family members.* (SOTHO)

Kwanyana (m) A little lamb. (SOTHO)

Kwatla (m) Be strong. (SOTHO)

Kwelama Follow in age or in order of birth. (NGUNI)

Kwelanga Of the sunshine. (NGUNI)

Kwelanwe Be heard. *This is when the prayer for the child was heard.* (SOTHO)

Kwele Neat person. (SOTHO)

Kwelego One who sensed. (SOTHO)

Kwelela An applause. (SOTHO)

Kwelwe Was heard. *This is when the prayer for the child was heard.* (SOTHO)

Kwemukela Accept with an open hand. (NGUNI)

Kwemvelo Of the nature. (NGUNI)

Kwena Be strong and established. (SOTHO)

Kwenaba Be comfortable. (NGUNI)

Kwenama (f) Our happiness. *Such a name refers to the atmosphere that surrounded the cradle at the birth of the bearer.* (NGUNI)

Kwenele (f) It is enough. *The birth of the child has brought fulfillment to the family.* (NGUNI)

Kwenelisa (f) Being fulfilled. (NGUNI)

Kwenza A deed done. (NGUNI)

Kwenzekile It has already happened. (NGUNI)

Kwenzokuhle Doer of good deeds. (NGUNI)

Kwesiso Understanding. (SOTHO)

Kweswa Kwetse Kwewa Be heard. *This is when the prayer for the child was heard.* (SOTHO)

Kwete One who surpasses others in strength. (SOTHO)

Kwetsaba Be excited. (NGUNI)

Kwetsamela Stretch out and relax in the sunshine. (NGUNI)

Kwetsembeka Be faithful and reliable. (NGUNI)

Kwetsima Holiness. (XITSONGA)

Kwezi (f) The early morning star. (NGUNI)

Kwezizwe Of the nations. *May be given to a child whose father is of another nationality.* (NGUNI)

Kwile Heard. *This is when the prayer for the child was heard.* (SOTHO)

L'a-baka-kambirhi Beating twice. *A praise name; almost the equivalent meaning as 'hitting two birds with one stone.'* (XITSONGA)

Laana Instruct one another. (SOTHO)

Labalabelo Desire earnestly. (SOTHO)

Labobedi Born on Thursday. (SOTHO)

Laborari Born on Wednesday. (SOTHO)

Laboratora Born on Saturday. (SOTHO)

Laela Educate. *Such a name conveys the values and expectations of the name-giver.* (SOTHO)

Laiwa Be educated. *Such a name conveys the values and expectations of the name-giver.* (SOTHO)

Lakaetsa Congratulate. *This name invites others to join in the celebration of the birth of this child.* (SOTHO)

Lakasela Glow; glitter. *Blessing declaration.* (SOTHO)

Lalamisa The tolerant person. *The name-giver may be expressing her response to a particular situation in her marriage.* (NGUNI) (BASOTHO)

Lalediwe (f) The invited one. *The family has been looking forward to the birth of the child.* (SOTHO)

Lalelayo (f) The obedient one. (NGUNI)

Laletsa (f) To invite. *Such a name reflects that the parent had prepared for the birth of the child.* (SOTHO)

Lamekile (f) One who has appeared suddenly. *Such a name suggests that this might have been an unplanned pregnancy.* (NGUNI)

Lamulile (f) **Lamla** (m) Peacemaker. *The one who intervenes to make peace between two opposing sides. The name-giver believes that the birth of a child will bring about reconciliation within the home.* (NGUNI)

Lamthuthu Battery chicken. *Nickname for someone shy.* (NGUNI)

Landelana Landela Landelisa (f) Follow another one; follow; cause to follow. *The name is based on the order of birth.* (NGUNI)

Landelwa (f) One who is being followed. *The name is based on the order of birth.* (NGUNI)

Landisa (f) Narrate a story or an event. *The birth of a child may be a constant reminder of a certain event in the family.* (NGUNI)

Landiwe (f) The one who has been brought back to where they belong. (NGUNI)

Langa (m) Bright as the sun. (NGUNI)

Langalakhe (m) His light. (NGUNI)

Langalamalanga (m) The great day that surpasses other days. (NGUNI)

Langalethu (m) Our sunshine. (NGUNI)

Langalibalele (m) The sun is blazing hot. (NGUNI)

Langanani (m) Choice. (XITSONGA)

Langelihle (m) It is a beautiful day. (NGUNI)

Langutani You must observe. (XITSONGA)

Langutisa Take care of. (XITSONGA)

Lapeng Come home. *This may be a political name, summoning those in exile.* (SOTHO)

Lapolosa Refresh; revive; cause to rest. (SOTHO)

Latani Throwing something. *Protective name for a child born after successive infant deaths.* (TSHIVENDA)

Lavhelesani Be an onlooker. *Advice not to get involved with what is going on, usually with regard to a discord.* (TSHIVENDA)

Lawula (m) Judge. (NGUNI)

Lawula (m) Pacify. (XITSONGA)

Lazola Quiet. *From the expression 'ilizwe lazola': the nation is quiet.* (NGUNI)

Leba la ka My pigeon. (SOTHO)

Lebaka Motivation. (SOTHO)

Lebalêla Forgive; pardon. (SOTHO)

Lebana Look at each other. (SOTHO)

Lebelisa Worthy of admiration. (SOTHO)

Lebella Anticipate. (SOTHO)

Lebelo Speedily accomplished. (SOTHO)

Lebenya Highly prized. (SOTHO)

Lebeola (m) Barber. *Name that depicts the name-giver's trade or talents.* (SOTHO)

Lebo Thanks. *Sometimes used as a short name for 'Lebohang'.* (SOTHO)

Leboga (m) A gift given as a token of gratitude. (SOTHO)

Lebogang (m) Be thankful. (SOTHO)

Lebogela (m) Award granted in recognition of excellence. (SOTHO)

Leboha (m) An expression of gratitude. (SOTHO)

Lebohang (m) Be thankful. (SOTHO)

Lebona (m) The one who sees. (SOTHO)

Lebosega (m) One who deserves thanks. (SOTHO)

Lebotse Beautiful. (SOTHO)

Lechabile The sun has risen. (SOTHO)

Lechatla Living in peace. (SOTHO)

Ledima The thunderstorm. (SOTHO)

Ledume An earnest longing or desire. (SOTHO)

Leeto This name can be for a child born on a journey. (SOTHO)

Lefa (m) Heritage; inheritance. (SOTHO)

Leferefere (m) A deceitful person. (SOTHO)

Lehana (m) One who-refuses. *Recital name given to himself by the initiate for his praise poem.* (SOTHO)

Lehlasedi (m) A sunbeam. (SOTHO)

Lehlohonolo (m) Luck; blessing. (SOTHO)

Lehumi (m)   Wealth. (SOTHO)

Lehumo (m)   Riches; wealth. (SOTHO)

Lehupela (f)   A flower budding. (SOTHO)

Leitamo   Admiration. (TSHIVENDA)

Leitibolo (m)   The oldest child in the family. (SOTHO)

Leitsibulo (m)   My first-born. (SOTHO)

Lekana (m)   Be equal; be sufficient for; be enough. (SOTHO)

Lekanago (m)   Which are equal; which are sufficient for; which are enough. (SOTHO)

Lekanang (m)   We now have enough. (SOTHO)

Lekane (m)   Equal; sufficient; enough. (SOTHO)

Lekanego (m)   Which is equal/sufficient/enough. (SOTHO)

Lekanyetsa (m)   We are grateful. (SOTHO)

Lekaota (m)   Of the famine. *Originated from the word 'Bokaota' meaning famine.* (SOTHO)

Lekelela (m)   Help out. *The name-giver may use the naming of the child as an opportunity to solicit help in a situation where direct communication will not be appropriate.* (NGUNI)

Lekgotla (m)   Court of law. *Refers to social disharmony amongst the relatives.* (SOTHO)

Lekhotla (m)   *See 'Lekgotla'.*

Lekona (m)   Has sufficed. (SOTHO)

Lelaka (m) Sun. *Archaic* (SOTHO)

Leleka (m) Follow a path or pursue. (SOTHO)

Lelethu It is ours. *From the political expression, 'Lelizwe lelethu': This is our land.* (NGUNI)

Lemohang Lemoha (m) Take cognizance. (SOTHO)

Lemukani (m) Take care. (XITSONGA)

Lenepa (m) One who hits the target. *Recital name given to himself by the initiate for his praise poem.* (SOTHO)

Lenhle (f) The beautiful one. (NGUNI)

Lenka Taker. (SOTHO)

Lensha The new one. (NGUNI)

Leoatle Ocean. *The child may have been born in a place near the ocean.* (SOTHO)

Lepolesa (m) Police officer. *Name that depicts the name-giver's trade or talents.* (SOTHO)

Lepoqo (m) Dispute. *Moshoeshoe's real name. Moshoeshoe was the founder of the Basotho nation. His name is a historic name, recording an event that happened when he was born.* (SOTHO)

Leraho Gentle. (TSHIVENDA)

Lerata (f) Noisy one. (BASOTHO)

Leratano (f) Mutual love. (SOTHO)

Lerato (f) Love. *The child is viewed as the product of the love between the mother and the father.* (SOTHO)

Lereko (f) Compassion. (SOTHO)

Lerose (f) A cluster of berries. (SOTHO)

Lerothodi (f) Raindrop. *The child was born when it was raining.* (SOTHO)

Lerumo The one in the lead; ahead of others. (SOTHO)

Leruo Possessing valuables. (SOTHO)

Lesea New born baby. *Can be used to address the baby before it is officially named.* (SOTHO)

Lesedi (f) Light; illumination. (SOTHO)

Lesego (f) Blessed. (SOTHO)

Leseli (f) Light; illumination. (SOTHO)

Lesetja (m) Character name. *These are the names usually given to initiates when they are going through the initiation school.* (SOTHO)

Lesetsa (m) Forgive. *Traditional folktale name.* (SOTHO)

Lesika (m) Relative. *The mother and the father may be distant relatives (endogamy).* (SOTHO)

Lesoboro (m) Youth. (SOTHO)

Lesokelo (m) Compassion. (SOTHO)

Lesokgola A baby who seldom cries. (SOTHO)

Lesoko Compassion. (SOTHO)

Leswalo Favourite. (SOTHO)

Letago Glory; triumphant honour. (SOTHO)

Lethabo Delight. (SOTHO)

Lethabong In his or her joy. (SOTHO)

Lethekga Support; prop up; sustain. (SOTHO)

Lethinhlanhla The one who brings luck. (NGUNI)

Lethinjabulo The joy bringer. (NGUNI)

Lethiwe (f) Been brought. (NGUNI)

Lethizibusiso The one who comes with blessings. (NGUNI)

Lethokuhle The bringer of excellent things. (NGUNI)

Lethukuthula The one who brings peace. (NGUNI)

Lethumasa (f) Uninitiated girl. (SOTHO)

Lethumusa The grace bringer. (NGUNI)

Lethuthando The one who brings love. (NGUNI)

Lethuxolo Bringer of forgiveness. (NGUNI)

Letlama (m) One who unites. *Recital name given to himself by the initiate for his praise poem.* (SOTHO)

Letlana Love each other. (SOTHO)

Letlanya Restore peace. (SOTHO)

Letlega Be fortunate. *This is a blessing pronouncement.* (SOTHO)

Letleke A wealthy one. (SOTHO)

Letlotlo Treasure. (SOTHO)

Letsatsi Sun; day. (SOTHO)

Letsekha (m) Born in the Matsekheng area. (SOTHO)

Letshego Laughter. (SOTHO)

Letshwao Impact; significance. (SOTHO)

Letsibolo The oldest child in the family. (SOTHO)

Letsididi May you be blessed. *This is a blessing pronouncement.* (SOTHO)

Letsie (f) Name of Basotho chief. (SOTHO)

Letuka (f) He who causes problems. *Name from a praise poem.* (SOTHO)

Lewatle (f) Ocean. *The child may have been born near the sea.* (SOTHO)

Liboko Praises. (SOTHO)

Liduka (f) Royal girls. *Name which was given to the girls of Cetswayo's kraal.* (NGUNI)

Liepollo Revelations; exposures. (SOTHO)

Lihle It is beautiful. (NGUNI)

Likhang Arguments. (SOTHO)

Likhaya This one is our home. *From the belief that a child makes a home.* (NGUNI)

Likongotlo The spine; the vine stick. (XITSONGA)

Limakatso Surprises; amazements. (SOTHO)

Limpho Gifts; presents. (SOTHO)

Linda To wait. *Also short form of 'Lindani', 'Lindelwa', 'Lindile', 'Lindiwe'.* (NGUNI)

Lindani Wait patiently. (NGUNI)

Linde Short form of 'Lindelani'. (TSHIVENDA)

Lindela Wait for. (NGUNI)

Lindelani (m) Wait patiently. (TSHIVENDA)

Lindeleka (f) Have been expected. (NGUNI)

Lindelwa (f) We are waiting. (NGUNI)

Lindeni What are you waiting for? (NGUNI)

Lindi (f) Short form of 'Lindiwe'. (NGUNI)

Lindile (f) *See 'Lindelwa'.*

Lindinkosi Waiting on the Lord. (NGUNI)

Lindisa (f) Make wait for. *This name can be given where there was delayed labour.* (NGUNI)

Lindiwe We have been waiting for her. (NGUNI)

Lindokuhle Lindo Waiting for what is good. *Combination of 'Linda' and 'Kuhle'.* (NGUNI)

Lineo Gifts; talents. (SOTHO)

Lintle (f) Beauty. (SOTHO)

Lioli (m) Golden eagle. *Name given to someone born in the Berea district.* (SOTHO)

Lipalesa (f) Flowers. (SOTHO)

Lisebo Whispers. (SOTHO)

Liso It is the eye. (NGUNI)

Litha The light. (NGUNI)

Litseho Laughter. (SOTHO)

Litsehoana Little laughter. (SOTHO)

Litsoanelo Suitable things. (SOTHO)

Livhuna Be thankful. (TSHIVENDA)

Livhuwani Livhu Acknowledgement; being grateful. (TSHIVENDA)

Liyandza Increase. (NGUNI)

Lizane A contribution. (NGUNI)
Lizeka (f) A present. (NGUNI)
Lizo A gift. (NGUNI)
Lizwi The voice. (NGUNI)
Lolama (f) Assume the correct order. (SOTHO)
Lolita (f) The light. (NGUNI)
Lomalungelo (f) *See 'Nomalungelo'.*
Lomathemba (f) One with hope. (NGUNI)
Lombukiso (f) Our show. (NGUNI)
Lomkhosi (f) Born on the celebration day. (NGUNI)
Lomso (f) This special day; celebrating the birth. (NGUNI)
Londeka (f) The one who is kept safe. (NGUNI)
Londekile (f) One who has been safely kept. (NGUNI)
Londi (f) Short form of 'Londeka'. (NGUNI)
Londisizwe Preserve the nation. (NGUNI)
Londoloza To keep safe. (NGUNI)
Lonwabo Joyous; glad. (NGUNI)
Lopologa Lopologile Become free; be redeemed/rescued. (SOTHO)
Lotlegela Tell the news; inform. (SOTHO)
Lova (m) The lazy one. (XITSONGA)
Loyiso (m) Delightful victory. (NGUNI)
Luba (f) Flower. (NGUNI)
Lubabalo (f) The grace of God. (NGUNI)

Lubalethu (f)　Our flower. (NGUNI)

Lubela (f)　Refuge. (XITSONGA)

Lubelihle (f)　Beautiful flower. (NGUNI)

Lufuno　Love. *See also 'Funanani'.* (TSHIVENDA)

Lugisani (m)　Fix it. *This name may refer to a tense situation in the home which the birth of the child might fix.* (TSHIVENDA)

Lugqwayimba (m)　Person with a slender, wiry body. (NGUNI)

Luka (m)　Luminous; white. *Sotho name of biblical origin, derived from Luke.* (SOTHO)

Lukaya (m)　Home. (NGUNI)

Lukhalo　It is still quite a distance. (NGUNI)

Lukhanyo　The light. (NGUNI)

Lula　Trouble-free and undisturbing. (NGUNI)

Lulama　Meek. (NGUNI)

Lulamela　Be obedient to. (NGUNI)

Lulamile　Stay in good health. (NGUNI)

Lulamisa　The meek or gentle one. (NGUNI)

Luleka　Must be advised. (NGUNI)

Lulekayo　The one who advises. (NGUNI)

Lulonke　The family is now complete. (NGUNI)

Lulu　Large. *Also used as a pet name or short form of 'Lungile', 'Lungelo'.* (NGUNI)

Luludzela　Sing a lullaby. (TSHIVENDA)

Lumeka Kindle. (NGUNI)

Lumka Beware. (NGUNI)

Lumkile Filled with wisdom and intelligence. (NGUNI)

Lunako Beauty. (TSHIVENDA)

Luncedo Our help. (NGUNI)

Lundi (m) Of the Lundi (Drakensberg) mountains. (NGUNI)

Lunga The good one. (NGUNI)

Lungalethu One of us. (NGUNI)

Lungalomndeni Family member. (NGUNI)

Lungani Be good. (NGUNI)

Lungelela Extend. *From the proverb 'ukuzala ukuzelungelela': when you give birth you are extending yourself. When your children help you, it is said that you have been extended.* (NGUNI)

Lungelo Right, privilege. (NGUNI)

Lungelwa (f) It is suitable. (NGUNI)

Lunghile (f) Goodness. (XITSONGA)

Lungile (f) Good. (NGUNI)

Lungisa (m) To put things right/ in order. (NGUNI)

Lungisile Lungi (m) She has corrected things. (NGUNI)

Lungiswa (m) One who has been made right. (NGUNI)

Lungu To peep. (NGUNI)

Luntu Mankind. (NGUNI)

Luphumlo It is the one who will bring rest. (NGUNI)

Lusanda (f)   The family is still increasing. (NGUNI)

Lusapho   Children; descendants. (NGUNI)

Lusi   Short form of 'Malusi'. (NGUNI)

Lutendo   Belief; faith. (TSHIVENDA)

Lutfo   At least we have something. (NGUNI)

Luthando   It is love. (NGUNI)

Lutsandvo   By means of love. (NGUNI)

Luvelo   The sympathetic one. (NGUNI)

Luvhani   Pay homage to. (TSHIVENDA)

Luvhengo   Hatred. *This name, with its negative connotations, is given in order to protect the child against the evil eye.* (TSHIVENDA)

Luviwe   We have been heard. *The prayer for the child has been heard.* (NGUNI)

Luvo   One's opinion or idea. (NGUNI)

Luvuyo   *See 'Vuyo'.* (NGUNI)

Luxolo   *See 'Daluxolo'.* (NGUNI)

Luyanda   *See 'Ayanda'.* (NGUNI)

Luyolo   Give instruction. (NGUNI)

Luzuko   The gracious one. (NGUNI)

Lwanda   Increase. (NGUNI)

Lwandile   They have increased. (NGUNI)

Lwandisa (f)   *See 'Andisa'.*

Lwandisile (f)   *See 'Andile'.*

Lwandisiwe (f)   They have been increased. (NGUNI)

Lwandiso (m) *See 'Andile'.*
Lwandlekazi (f) Of the sea. (NGUNI)
Lwazi Knowledge. (NGUNI)
Lwazilwabo Their knowledge. (NGUNI)
Lwazilwakhe His knowledge. (NGUNI)
Lwazoluhle Intelligent one. (NGUNI)

Maanda One with power/strength. (TSHIVENDA)

Maandandiawe It is God's power. (TSHIVENDA)

Maatla (m) Power; strength. (SOTHO)

Ma-ba-a-hleka Mabahleka (m) The one who beats while laughing. *This name can be used to refer to one with subtle cruelty. The name-giver may use such a name to expose such a person within the home.*

Mabandla (m) One belonging to all. *The child does not belong to the parents only, but to the whole clan and community.* (NGUNI)

Mabannda (m) One who trades with belts. *Name that depicts the name-giver's trade or talents.* (TSHIVENDA)

Ma-ba-xifuva (m) The one who touches the heart. (XITSONGA)

Mabhalangozipho (m) One who writes with their nails. *Name for an educated person.* (NGUNI)

Mabhelandile (m) The clan of 'Amabhele' has increased. (NGUNI)

Mabihana (m) The ugly one. *This is a protective name to shield the child from the evil eye.* (XITSONGA)

Mabihanyana (m) The little ugly one. *This is a protective name to shield the child from the evil eye.* (XITSONGA)

Mabohlale (m) Wisdom. (SOTHO)

Mabongi (f) *See 'Abonga'.*

Mabongwandile (m)   The family of Mabongwa has increased. *A combination of 'Mabongwa' and 'Andile'.* (NGUNI)

Mabotse (f)   Beautiful (ones). (SOTHO)

Mabutfo (m)   Soldiers. (NGUNI)

Mabuto (m)   Warrior. (NGUNI)

Madala (m)   The very old one. (XITSONGA)

Madandume (m)   Name of former Botswana chief. (SOTHO)

Madevana (m)   Nickname for someone with a small moustache. (NGUNI)

Madira (f)   Mother of enemies. (SOTHO)

Madlodlombiya (m)   Nickname for one with untidy hair. (NGUNI)

Madoda (m)   Men. (NGUNI)

Madodenzani (m)   What are the men doing? *This name can be given when there has been a fight amongst the men of the home.* (NGUNI)

Madodonke (m)   All the men. *Name given when all the children are boys.* (NGUNI)

Madolanzima (m)   The unenthusiastic one. (NGUNI)

Maduvha (m)   Days. (TSHIVENDA)

Madyisambitsi (m)   One who persists in hurting others. (XITSONGA)

Mafanato (m) One who dies with them (secrets). *Meaning one who will not disclose a secret matter.* (XITSONGA)

Mafatla (m) Old age wisdom. (SOTHO)

Mafatle (m) *Probably adapted from 'Mafatla' which means: 'a bald head showing old age and wisdom'.* (SOTHO)

Mafavuke (m) One who survives great trouble. (NGUNI)

Mafika (m) The one who has arrived. (NGUNI)

Mafikajwayele (m) One who easily adjusts to change. (NGUNI)

Mafikizolo (m) The one who has just arrived. (NGUNI)

Mafu (m) Cloud. *For a child born on a cloudy day.* (NGUNI)

Mafukuzela (m) The one who carries a burden. (NGUNI)

Mafundafobele (m) One who learns and quickly takes in information. *Name given to a venturesome man.* (NGUNI)

Mafundanezibi (m) *Nickname given for a credulous person.*

Mafungwase (f) **Mafungwashe** (f) By whom they swear (funga). *Name given to an older sister in the family.* (NGUNI)

Mafushazana Short one. *Nickname for a short person.* (NGUNI)

Mafusini In the fallow fields. *Name based on the place where the mother gave birth.* (XITSONGA)

Magangane (m) The naughty one. (NGUNI)

Magebandile (m) The Zulu family has increased. (NGUNI)

Magimani (m) The short one. (XITSONGA)

Magqamehlezi (f) The one who looks attractive only when sitting down. *Nickname for a person with a beautiful face but ugly figure.* (NGUNI)

Magudumeja One doing things forcefully and swiftly. (NGUNI)

Magugu Precipitation. (XITSONGA)

Magumisana One putting dry food in their mouth with nothing to wash it down. *The mother may use such a name as a grievance about the poverty in the home.* (XITSONGA)

Magwazayiqhube One who carries a deed to completion. (NGUNI)

Magwazendlini (m) One who makes enemies among his homefolk. *In this case, the name was taken from the praise poem for a man who married a girl that his brother was also interested in.* (NGUNI)

Magwazephindele (m) One who is never satisfied with a single achievement. (NGUNI)

Magwembeni (m) At the time of the goat's disease. *This event marks the time of the birth.* (XITSONGA)

Mahahele (m) The one who goes here and there. (XITSONGA)

Mahamba edwa (m) The one who walks alone. (XITSONGA)

Mahamba (m) The one who likes to travel. (NGUNI)

Mahambanendlwana (m) The one who travels with his/her house i.e. nomads. (NGUNI)

Mahehe (m) The mute. (XITSONGA)

Mahetelelo (m) End. *Last child born in the family.* (XITSONGA)

Mahlahle (m) Morning star. (XITSONGA)

Mahlahluvana (m) The little bone thrower. *This name refers to witchdoctors.* (XITSONGA)

Mahlalahleka (m) One who is constantly laughing. *Nickname for a sweet-spirited person.* (NGUNI)

Mahlale (m) Wisdom. (SOTHO)

Mahlaphahlapha One who is untidy. (NGUNI)

Mahlapholane Morning star. (SOTHO)

Mahlathini (m) Of the forest. *Also used for a man who does not shave his beard.* (NGUNI)

Mahlatse Witness. (XITSONGA)

Mahlekehlatsini (m) One laughing inside the forest. *Usually given to a heavily bearded man.* (NGUNI)

Mahlodi (m) Born during a time of mourning in the family. (SOTHO)

Mahlomulo (m) Sufferings. *This name may be used to express a variety of grievances.* (XITSONGA)

Mahlori (m) Miracle. *May be given to a child born after a long time of trying to conceive.* (XITSONGA)

Mahlubandile (m) The family of 'Mahlubi' has increased. *A combination of 'Mahlubi' and 'Andile'.* (NGUNI)

Mahlubi (m) Of the 'Mahlubi' clan. (NGUNI)

Mahluleli (m) The judge. (NGUNI)

Mahluli (m) Victor. *This name can be given to a child whose chances of living were against the odds.* (NGUNI)

Mahlweni-ka-tintswalo (m) Kindness in the eyes (only). *This is an idiomatic expression suggesting that someone only pretends to be your friend.* (XITSONGA)

Mahumô (m) Riches; different sorts of wealth. (SOTHO)

Mahunisi (m) The one who acts as if he did not hear. (XITSONGA)

Majaha (m) Young men. (XITSONGA)

Majikanelanga One who turns with the sunshine. *Usually a nickname for a lazy person who prefers basking in the sun the whole day to working.* (NGUNI)

Majolandile (m) The family of 'AmaMajola' has increased. *A combination of 'Majola' and 'Andile'.* (NGUNI)

Makakaramba (m) Small strong boy. (NGUNI)

Makalo (m) Perplexity; surprise; bewilderment. (SOTHO)

Makasela (m) The crawling one. (XITSONGA)

Makazi (f) My mother's sister. (NGUNI)

Makgolo (f) Grandmother. (SOTHO)

Makgotla (m) *See 'Lekgotla'.*

Makgotso (f) Mother of peace. (SOTHO)

Makhadzi (f) Paternal aunt. (TSHIVENDA)

Makhahlela (m) The kicker. *The child might have been kicking a lot whilst in the womb.* (XITSONGA)

Makhala (m) One who cries often. (NGUNI)

Makhamisa (m) One with the mouth always open. (NGUNI)

Makhelwane Neighbour. (NGUNI)

Makhenkesi (m) Traveller. (NGUNI)

Makhi The one who builds. *Name that depicts the name-giver's trade or talents.* (NGUNI)

Makhisizwe (m) One who builds the nation. (NGUNI)

Makholwa Believers. (NGUNI)

Makhosandile (m) The kings have increased. (NGUNI)

Makhosazana (f) Princesses. (NGUNI)

Makhosetive (m) The king of the land. *First name of the King of Swaziland, His Majesty King Makhosetive 'Ngwenyama' Mswati III.* (NGUNI)

Makhosi (m) One of the royals. *Also short form of 'Makhosazana'.* (NGUNI)

Makhosini (m) A prince; one of royalty. (NGUNI)

Makhosonke (m) All chiefs. (NGUNI)

Makhothama (m) One who bows. *One respectful to his seniors and who will keep bowing.* (NGUNI)

Makhotla (m) An alternative form of 'Makgotla'. (SOTHO)

Makhulu (f) Grandmother. (NGUNI)

Makhulu-tshinna (m) Father-in-law. (TSHIVENDA)

Makhulu-tshisadzi (f) Mother-in-law. (TSHIVENDA)

Makohlo The one who had not been thought of. *In the case of an unexpected pregnancy.* (XITSONGA)

Makoti (f) Newly-wedded bride. (NGUNI)

Makoti The vultures. *This is the same name used by the Nguni for the daughter-in-law.* (XITSONGA)

Makubenjalo Let it be so! (NGUNI)

Makulana The little tall one. (XITSONGA)

Makwavo Cousin. (XITSONGA)

Malahlanidzovo (m) Something to be thrown away with the skin. *That is, something not worth saving, usually said of dogs and donkeys. This is a protective name to shield the child from evil spirits.* (XITSONGA)

Malandela (m) The follower. (NGUNI)

Malebatja (m) He makes us forget the pain. (SOTHO)

Malebô (m) Aiming. (SOTHO)

Malebogô (m) Thanks; thanksgiving. (SOTHO)

Malefane (m) One who pays. (SOTHO)

Malehu (f) Mourning. *The child was born during a funeral in the family.* (SOTHO)

Malepfu (m) Beard. (XITSONGA)

Malesotho (f) Mother of Lesotho. (SOTHO)

Maletsatsi (f) Mother of day or sun. (SOTHO)

Malibongwe (m) May His (God's) name be praised. (NGUNI)

Maliwa (m) He who is rejected. *The child's father might deny his paternity.* (NGUNI)

Malokazana (f) Daughter-in-law. (NGUNI)

Maluleke (m) Advise him. (NGUNI)

Malume (m) Maternal uncle. (NGUNI)

Malumekazi (f) Maternal aunt. (NGUNI)

Malusi (m) The sheep tender; shepherd. *Name that depicts the name-giver's trade or talents.* (NGUNI)

Malwisi (m) The one who brings fights. (XITSONGA)

Mam'khulu (f) The older sister of my mother. (NGUNI)

Mam'ncane (f) The younger sister of my mother. (NGUNI)

Mama (f) Mother. (NGUNI)

Mamazane (f) Little girl. (NGUNI)

Mamêlêlô (f) Patience. (SOTHO)

Mamello Perseverance. (SOTHO)

Mamezala (f) My mother-in-law. (NGUNI)

Mamgobhozi (f) Overflowing. *A name given for the gossiper; for she always has something to tell.* (NGUNI)

Mamkhulu (f) Mother's older daughter. (NGUNI)

Mamncane (f) Mother's young daughter. (NGUNI)

Mamphasa (f) Flower. *See 'Palesa'.* (SOTHO)

Mampho (f) Greatest gift. (SOTHO)

Mamusi (f) Son of the pestle. (XITSONGA)

Manala (f) The wealthy one. *Born during the time of good harvest.* (NGUNI)

Manana (f) Mother; aunt. (XITSONGA)

Mananga (f) In the desert. *Name based on the place where the mother gave birth.* (XITSONGA)

Mancishana (f) The stingy one. *Usually a nickname for someone miserly.* (NGUNI)

Mandifunde Let me learn my lesson. (NGUNI)

Mandisa (f) The sweet one. (NGUNI)

Mandisi (f) The one who causes an increase. (NGUNI)

Mandla (m) One with power or strength. *The strength in the family has been increased by the birth of the child.* (NGUNI)

Mandlakayise (m) Strength of his father. *The child will strengthen his father.* (NGUNI)

Mandlakazi (m) Most powerful. (NGUNI)

Mandlethu (m) Our power. (NGUNI)

Manduleli (m) A leader; one who goes before others; a forerunner. (NGUNI)

Mane (f) They (the children) are four. (NGUNI)

Maneli (m) Minister of the gospel. *Name that depicts the name-giver's trade or talents* (NGUNI)

Manelisi (m)   The one who satisfies. (NGUNI)

Manesi (f)   Mild and gentle. (NGUNI)

Manga (m)   Short form of 'Simangaliso'. (NGUNI)

Mangalisa (m)   She has surprised us. (NGUNI)

Mangalisiwe (f)   Has been surprised. (NGUNI)

Mangaliso (m)   A miracle. *A child born after waiting to conceive for a long time.* (NGUNI)

Mangungwana (m)   The little short and plump one. (NGUNI)

Mangwayana (m)   The little clever one. (XITSONGA)

Manqoba (m)   The conqueror. (NGUNI)

Mantele   Mama, look after me. (SOTHO)

Mantfombi (f)   Girl. (NGUNI)

Mantombazana (f)   Girls. *When there are only girls in the family.* (NGUNI)

Mantsopa (f)   *Name of one of the female leaders in the history of the Basotho.*

Mantwa (f)   Mother of war, one who likes fighting. (SOTHO)

Manyanisi (f)   One who unites. (NGUNI)

Maondza-qinile (m)   Thin but strong. (XITSONGA)

Mapahla   Second born identical twin. (XITSONGA)

Mapatweni On the road. *A woman will name a child this when she has been accused of committing adultery. She does this to show that she is not afraid to face the accusation.* (XITSONGA)

Maphavuma One jumping and leaping like a frog. (NGUNI)

Maphefo (f) She was born when it was windy. (SOTHO)

Maphika (m) The one who refuses. Also short form of 'Maphikelela', 'Mphikeleli'. (NGUNI)

Maphikelela (m) **Mphikeleli** (m) Persistent; persevering. (NGUNI)

Mapula (f) She was born when it was raining. (SOTHO)

Maqhubandaba (m) One who relays the story. (NGUNI)

Maqinase (f) Traditional name from a tale about a naughty piglet. (NGUNI)

Mareka (m) Polite; shining. *Sotho name of biblical origin, derived from Mark.* (SOTHO)

Marhandzateka One who always wants to receive without making an effort. (XITSONGA)

Marhumbini In the ruins. *Name based on the place where the mother gave birth.* (XITSONGA)

Maria (f) Rebellion. *Sotho name of biblical origin, derived from Mary.* (SOTHO)

Marubini (m) A place used for farming. (TSHIVENDA)

Masabatha (f) Daughter of the Sabbath. (NGUNI)

Masala (f) The one who remained behind. *During childbirth the mother died, leaving the baby behind.* (TSHIVENDA)

Masana (f) The breaking of day; sunrise. (XITSONGA)

Masana-A-Tshilidzi (f) The rays of the grace of God. (TSHIVENDA)

Masande (f) Let us increase. (NGUNI)

Masasana (f) The little nice one. (XITSONGA)

Masase (f) Morning star. (TSHIVENDA)

Masaswivona (f) One who continues to see them (troubles). (XITSONGA)

Masego (f) Blessings. (SOTHO)

Mashesha (m) The one who is always in a hurry. (NGUNI)

Mashilo (m) Fooled by girls. *Name given to a boy in the midst of girls in the family.* (SOTHO)

Mashudu (m) Lucky. (TSHIVENDA)

Masibonge (m) Let us give thanks. (NGUNI)

Masila (m) He grinds with the grinding stone. (SOTHO)

Masingita Creative miracles. *The name can be given where the conception was difficult.* (XITSONGA)

Masiphilile If we are still alive. *The hope of the name-giver to live long, but the expression has connotations of life and death being beyond human control.* (NGUNI)

Masirheni Graveyard. *When the mother has lost a number of children successively, a surviving one will be given such a name to make them unacceptable to the messenger of death.* (XITSONGA)

Masiya The remnant. *Possibly a name of the last-born child, usually if all the other children are already grown up.* (XITSONGA)

Masiza One who is always helpful. (NGUNI)

Masonto (f) Born on Sunday. (NGUNI)

Masopha (m) The name of the son of Moshoeshoe, a former Sotho Chief. (SOTHO)

Masovori (m) The one of the pepperbush. (XITSONGA)

Masunga (m) Name of former Botswana chief. (SOTHO)

Masungini (m) In the huts of the circumcision. (XITSONGA)

Masupha (m) *See 'Masopha'.*

Masusamalanga Masusamalenge The wiper of eye's secretions. *Name for one who has been long awaited.* (XITSONGA)

Maswabi Regret; shame. *This name may be associated with teenage pregnancy or a child conceived as a result of a rape.* (SOTHO)

Maswazi Of the Swazis. (NGUNI)

Masweu Good. (SOTHO)

Mateboho (f) Mother of gratitude. (SOTHO)

Mathabo (f) Happiness; joy. (SOTHO)

Mathanda (f) One who loves. (NGUNI)

Mathapelo (f) Prayerful woman or mother of person called Thapelo. *See also 'Thapelo'.* (SOTHO)

Mathatha (m) Moustache. (XITSONGA)

Mathemba (f) One with trust. (NGUNI)

Mathokoza (f) One who delighted. (NGUNI)

Mathuba (f) Opportunities. (NGUNI)

Matimba Power. (XITSONGA)

Matimu History. (XITSONGA)

Matini In the water. *Name based on the place where the mother gave birth when she had gone to fetch water.* (XITSONGA)

Mativula First born child. (XITSONGA)

Matjhatjhametse The swift one. (SOTHO)

Matjhi One born in March. (NGUNI)

Matlafala Become strong/empowered. (SOTHO)

Matlakala Rubbish heap. *When the mother has lost a number of children successively, a surviving one will be given such a name to make her unacceptable to the messenger of death.* (SOTHO)

Matlale No use for you. *This is a protective name given to shield the child against misfortune meted out by evil spirits.* (XITSONGA)

Matlapulana (f) One who has come with rain. (SOTHO)

Matle (f) Admirable. (SOTHO)

Matlhari Matlharini (m) In the assegais storehouse. *Name based on the place where the mother gave birth.* (XITSONGA)

Matlho Eyes. (SOTHO)

Matli The one who comes. (SOTHO)

Matodzi Teardrops. *Generally refers to tears caused by death in the family. It is also a protective name used to shield the child from evil intentions.* (TSHIVENDA)

Matsale (f) Mother-in-law. (SOTHO)

Matsatsela The one who walks with little steps. (XITSONGA)

Matsela Someone who is always on the road looking for opportunity/greener pastures. (SOTHO)

Matseliso Consolation from mourning. (SOTHO)

Matshediso Matshidiso (f) Condolences. *Born soon after the death of a loved one.* (SOTHO)

Matshepo (f) Mother of hope. (SOTHO)

Matshwenyego (f) Suffering. (SOTHO)

Matsimela (f) The roots are firm. (TSHIVENDA)

Matsuvi The sad one. (XITSONGA)

Mattheu (m) Given; a reward. *Sotho name of biblical origin, derived from Matthew.* (SOTHO)

Matyala (m) The guilty one. (NGUNI)

Mavela (m) Has appeared. (NGUNI)

Mavhungu (m) Big worms. *Meaning the worms are also waiting for this one. This name is given to a child born after successive deaths in the family.* (TSHIVENDA)

Mavi (m) Words. (NGUNI)

Mawiliza (m) One who speaks incoherently. (NGUNI)

Mawolume (m) Maternal uncle. (NGUNI)

Mawuwani July. *Name given to a child born in July.* (XITSONGA)

Maxangweni (m) Poor sadness. (XITSONGA)

Maxisana (m) Deceiver. (XITSONGA)

Maziphula (m) The uprooter. (NGUNI)

Mazozo *Short form for 'Zolani', 'Zoleka', 'Zodwa'.* (NGUNI)

Mazwanzima (m) Hard words. (NGUNI)

Mazwi (m) Words. (NGUNI)

Mbalenhle (f) A beautiful flower. (NGUNI)

Mbali (f) Flower. (NGUNI)

Mbaliyami (f) My flower. (NGUNI)

Mbaliyethu (f) Our Flower. (NGUNI)

Mbalizothando (f) Flowers of love. (NGUNI)

Mbatjazwa (m) Exclaimed one. *Mother and father were distant cousins and Nguni culture does not allow endogamy, therefore the society had exclaimed that the parents defied this culture by getting married and having children.* (NGUNI)

Mbavhi (m) *Short form of 'Azwimmbavhi'.*

Mbeko (m) One with respect. (NGUNI)

Mbenyana (m)　The little handle. (XITSONGA)

Mbewulane (m)　The swallow. (XITSONGA)

Mbhali (f)　Flower. (NGUNI)

Mbhekeni (m)　Look to him. (NGUNI)

Mbhekwa (m)　The one they are looking up to for hope. (NGUNI)

Mbhoni　The witness. (XITSONGA)

Mbhuri　Grace. (XITSONGA)

Mbijana　Little. (NGUNI)

Mbiketeli　One who foretells. (NGUNI)

Mbilu　Heart. *The name-giver gave this name because there were love issues surrounding the birth of this child.* (TSHIVENDA)

Mbilwana　Little heart. (XITSONGA)

Mbitsi　Bitterness. *The name-giver may be reflecting on her bitter life experiences.* (XITSONGA)

Mbitsimuni　What kind of bitterness? *The name-giver may be reflecting on her bitter life experiences.* (XITSONGA)

Mbizeni (m)　He must be called; call him. (NGUNI)

Mbizo (m)　One born when there was an 'imbizo' (royal meeting). (NGUNI)

Mbofho　Mbo (m)　Free. (TSHIVENDA)

Mbofholowo (m)　Freedom. (TSHIVENDA)

Mboneni (m)　Behold him. (NGUNI)

Mbongeni (m)　Praise him. (NGUNI)

Mboniswa One with revelations. (NGUNI)

Mbonomuhle The optimistic one, full of good ideas. (NGUNI)

Mbopha (m) Imprison. (NGUNI)

Mboweni (m) In the leaves of the mbowa (calabash) tree. *Name based on the place where the mother gave birth when she went to gather wood.* (XITSONGA)

Mbudziso (m) Question. (TSHIVENDA)

Mbuedzedzo (m) Replacement. *When one child passes away, the next one can be viewed as the replacement.* (TSHIVENDA)

Mbukelwa (m) The one who is for showing. (NGUNI)

Mbula (m) Short form of 'Mbulaheni'. (TSHIVENDA)

Mbulawa (m) The one to be killed. *This is a protective name given in order to shield the child from evil intentions/spirits.* (NGUNI)

Mbulelo Thanks. (NGUNI)

Mbulwa Meek/quiet person. (XITSONGA)

Mburhi Handsome one. (XITSONGA)

Mburi Beautiful one. (XITSONGA)

Mbuso (m) Kingdom. (NGUNI)

Mbusowakhe (m) His kingdom. (NGUNI)

Mbuyi (m) Short form of 'Nombuyiselo'. (NGUNI)

Mbuyiseli (m) One who restores. (NGUNI)

Mbuyiselo (m) Restoration. (NGUNI)

Mbuyisi (m) Restorer. (NGUNI)

Mbuzeni (m) Ask him. *Such a name is a result of some or other incident in the homestead which has resulted in queries.* (NGUNI)

Mbuzo (m) The questionable one. *In a society in which men go away to work in the mines, the birthdate of the child must correspond with the date of the husband's last visit; if not, questions will be asked about its paternity.* (NGUNI)

Mcanukelwa (m) One they are annoyed with. *The name-giver was registering the behaviour of the in-laws towards her.* (NGUNI)

Mcathama (m) One who walks slowly on tip toes. (NGUNI)

Mcebisi (m) An adviser. (NGUNI)

Mcebo (m) Wealth. (NGUNI)

Mdelwa (m) The rejected one. (NGUNI)

Mdingi (m) One who lacks. *In this case, the father had just lost his job.* (NGUNI)

Mduduzi (m) The one who comforts/consoles. (NGUNI)

Mdunyelwa (m) Famous one. (NGUNI)

Mebotse (f) Beautiful. (SOTHO)

Mehlo Face or eyes. (NGUNI)

Mehlomane One with four eyes. *Nickname for one wearing glasses.* (NGUNI)

Mehluli (m) Victor. (NGUNI)

Melikhaya (m) One who stands for the home. (NGUNI)

Melinto (m) One who stands for something. (NGUNI)

Melisizwe (m) One who stands for the nation. (NGUNI)

Melusi (m) Shepherd. (NGUNI)

Membathisi (m) The one who clothes the other; one who covers one's nakedness. (NGUNI)

Mendiswa (f) One who has been wedded off. (NGUNI)

Menetjhani What do you mean? *In this case, the question is being directed at those who said that the mother was barren.* (NGUNI)

Mengwe (m) Name of former Botswana chief. (SOTHO)

Menônô Riches; fertility. (SOTHO)

Menzele (m) Do it for him. *The mother did not desire to have any more children, but still had more at the request of her husband.* (NGUNI)

Menzi (m) The creator. (NGUNI)

Mesatywa (m) Feared or revered one. (NGUNI)

Methembe (m) Trust in Him (God). (NGUNI)

Meyi (m) One born in May. (NGUNI)

Mfakelwa A foster child of a woman without a child. (NGUNI)

Mfana (m) Boy. (XITSONGA)

Mfanafuthi (m) It's a boy again. (NGUNI)

Mfanelo (m) What is fitting? (NGUNI)

Mfanimpela (m) It's truly a boy. (NGUNI)

Mfaniseni (m) One bearing resemblance. (NGUNI)

Mfazikazi (f) Worthy woman. (NGUNI)

Mfezeko Accomplishment. (NGUNI)

Mfezi The accomplisher. (NGUNI)

Mfihlelo One who has been kept secret. (NGUNI)

Mfiki Newcomer. (NGUNI)

Mfokisi (m) Spy; detective. (XITSONGA)

Mfolomani (m) Adapted from English 'foreman'. (NGUNI)

Mfowethu (m) My brother. (NGUNI)

Mfukuzeli (m) One who works hard. (NGUNI)

Mfundo (m) *See 'Nomfundo'.*

Mfuneko (m) He has been desired. (NGUNI)

Mfungelwa (m) One who has been threatened. (NGUNI)

Mfusi (m) A single child, succeeding twins. (NGUNI)

Mfuzile (m) One who resembles the other. (NGUNI)

Mfuzo (m) One who resembles. (NGUNI)

Mgagameli (m) An overreaching person. (NGUNI)

Mgagathwa (m) One who has been trained. (NGUNI)

Mgcineni (m) Keep him safe. (NGUNI)

Mgcineni (m) Take care of him. (NGUNI)

Mgcini (m) Keeper. (NGUNI)

Mgcinikababa (m) Father's keeper. (NGUNI)

Mgcobo (m) Rejoicing. (NGUNI)

Mgcotshwa (m) The anointed one. (NGUNI)

Mgqakhwe (m) An illegitimate child. (NGUNI)

Mgwabi (m) One who sings and chants. (NGUNI)

Mhakamuni (m) What manner of news is this? *Usually referring to bad news received at the time of birth.* (XITSONGA)

Mhambi (m) Traveller. (NGUNI)

Mhawu (m) Compassionate one. (NGUNI)

Mhawuri August. *Name given to a child born in August.* (XITSONGA)

Mhikana (f) The little barren one. *A woman gives this name to her child after hearing gossip that she is barren.* (XITSONGA)

Mhlaba (m) Of the earth. (NGUNI)

Mhlabunzima (m) The world is difficult. (NGUNI)

Mhlahlandlela (m) The one who paves the way. *Traditional folktale name.* (NGUNI)

Mhlakaza (m) The one who scattered. (NGUNI)

Mhlangane (m) Coming together. *Name of Dingane's (nineteenth century Zulu chief) brother.* (NGUNI)

Mhlanganisi (m) The one who brings together. (NGUNI)

Mhlekazi (m) Your Excellency! (NGUNI)

Mhleli (m) Planner. (NGUNI)

Mhletswa One who is gossiped about. *In this case, the mother used the name-giving as an opportunity to let the in-laws know that she is aware that they have been saying things behind her back.* (NGUNI)

Mhlobo My relation. (NGUNI)

Mhlonishwa (m) The honourable one. (NGUNI)

Mhlope The white one. *Name based on physical appearance.* (XITSONGA)

Mhluri (m) Prosperous. (XITSONGA)

Mhlwithi (m) Nickname given to a tall person. (NGUNI)

Mholi (m) The leader. (NGUNI)

Miditaba (f) Mother of controversy. (SOTHO)

Mihloti (m) Tears. (XITSONGA)

Mikea (m) Poor; humble. *Sotho name of biblical origin, derived from Micah.* (SOTHO)

Milisa (m) Cause to grow or bud. (NGUNI)

Miliswa (f) Rejuvenation. (NGUNI)

Minemandi (f) A nice day. (NGUNI)

Minenhle (f) A special day. (NGUNI)

Minenkulu (f) A big day. (NGUNI)

Minikazi (f) The great day. (NGUNI)

Minkateko Blessing. (XITSONGA)

Misingi The very large trees. (XITSONGA)

Mitarini How can you come on such a day? *The day of the birth may have coincided with the death of a relative or another misfortune in the family.* (XITSONGA)

Mitiro Acts. (XITSONGA)

Miyelani Keep quiet. (XITSONGA)

Mjabuliswa (f) One to be excited, pleased. (NGUNI)

Mjita (m) Nickname for a young man. (NGUNI)

Mkhango New and ready to be looked at. (NGUNI)

Mkhanyisi The one who ignites the light. (NGUNI)

Mkhetheni (m) Single him out. *In this case, the name was given to indicate conflict between the father of the child and his parents. The parents did not help him to pay the lobola for his bride, yet they did help his brothers.* (NGUNI)

Mkhohlisi (m) A deceiver. (NGUNI)

Mkhokheli (f) Leader; the one who gives guidance. (NGUNI)

Mkhoseli Sheltered. (NGUNI)

Mkhuhlane Disease. *Usually said of a sick child or one born with HIV.* (NGUNI)

Mkhuliseni (m) You must raise him. (NGUNI)

Mkhulu (m) Grandfather. (NGUNI)

Mkhululi (m) The liberator. (NGUNI)

Mkhuthali (m) Industrious one. (NGUNI)

Mkhuzeni (m) Warn him. *This name is a warning to someone within a society.* (NGUNI)

Mkhwenyana (m) Groom or son-in-law. (NGUNI)

Mkhwetha (m) An initiate. (NGUNI)

Mkolo (m) One who believes. (NGUNI)

Mkululi (m) The one who sets free. (NGUNI)

Mkuseli (m) The shelter. (NGUNI)

Mkutazi Mkuthazi (m) The encourager. (NGUNI)

Mlalandle (m) One who sleeps outside. (NGUNI)

Mlamli (m) The peacemaker. (NGUNI)

Mlawuli (m) The judge. (NGUNI)

Mlayedwa (m) He who fights alone. *The name-giver received no support during pregnancy.* (NGUNI)

Mlenzane (m) One leg. *This is also the name of a god that some of the Nguni believe in.* (NGUNI)

Mlethi (m) The one who brings. (NGUNI)

Mlilwana (m) Fiery one; hot-tempered one. (NGUNI)

Mlindeli The patient one. (NGUNI)

Mlindi One who waits. (NGUNI)

Mlingane Companion. (NGUNI)

Mlizo A present or gift. (NGUNI)

Mlokothwa (m) One who is untouchable. (NGUNI)

Mlondikhaya (m) The preserver of the home. (NGUNI)

Mlondisizwe (m) The preserver of the nation. (NGUNI)

Mlondolozi (m) Caretaker. (NGUNI)

Mlowo (m) Our blood relation. (NGUNI)

Mlulami (m) *See 'Lulama'.*

Mluleki (m) One who gives advice or counsel. (NGUNI)

Mlungiseleli (m) One who prepares ahead. (NGUNI)

Mlungisi (m) One who puts things right. (NGUNI)

Mlweli (m) The one who fights for me. (NGUNI)

Mlwisi (m) A helper in war; a fellow soldier. (NGUNI)

Mmaabo (f) She is their mother. (SOTHO)

Mmabatho (f) Mother of people. (SOTHO)

Mmadomi (f) Mother of independence. (SOTHO)

Mmakatsi (f) One who surprises. (SOTHO)

Mmakgônthê (f) Genuine. (SOTHO)

Mmalefa Mother of 'Lefa'. (SOTHO)

Mmalerato (f) Mother of 'Lerato'. (SOTHO)

Mmalesotho (f) Mother of Lesotho. (SOTHO)

Mmamogolo (f) Aunt; mother's elder sister. (SOTHO)

Mmamohau (f) Mother of mercy. (SOTHO)

Mmamoratwa (f) The beloved one. (SOTHO)

Mmane (f) Maternal aunt. (TSHIVENDA)

Mmangaleli (m) An accuser. (NGUNI)

Mmangalelwa (m) An accused. (NGUNI)

Mmanoga (m) Snake. *In this case, a snake frightened the mother while she was pregnant with the child.* (SOTHO)

Mmapalê (f) Good. (SOTHO)

Mmathapelo (f) Mother of prayer. *Also, mother of person called 'Thapelo'.* (SOTHO)

Mmatswale (f) Mother-in-law. (SOTHO)

Mmbangiseni (m) Fight against me. *A dispute-related name.* (VENDA) (TSONGA) (NGUNI)

Mmbavhi (m) Short form of 'Azwimmbavhi'. (TSHIVENDA)

Mmbengeni (m) Hate me. *A dispute-related name.* (TSHIVENDA)

Mmboneleni (m) Look after it for me. *Such a name can be given when the parents are old and they use the name to ask for help from relatives in raising the child.* (TSHIVENDA)

Mmbulaheni (m) Kill me. *This personal name is found in an environment where people are plotting to kill or have already killed someone. However, this personal name has a message of warning in it: should they decide to kill the name-giver, they will find people ready to defend the deceased.* (TSHIVENDA)

Mmbulungeni (m) Protect me. *Name given to request protection from those threatening the mother's life or that of a new born.* (TSHIVENDA)

Mmeli (m) Lawyer. (NGUNI)

Mmenyana (m) What is his name? (SOTHO)

Mmitsi (m) One who calls. (SOTHO)

Mmogedi (m) An onlooker. (SOTHO)

Mmolediswa The one who follows. *Given to a second born.* (SOTHO)

Mmolelwa The one talked about. (SOTHO)

Mmoloki Keeper; saviour. (SOTHO)

Mmonedi One who provides for. (SOTHO)

Mmoneng See him. *Name-giver is speaking to those who did not believe that the mother would give birth.* (SOTHO)

Mmotse (f) Beautiful. (SOTHO)

Mmusa Merciful and gentle one. (SOTHO)

Mmusi Governor. (SOTHO)

Mna Me. *Shows the individuality of the child.* (NGUNI)

Mnandisa (f) Make pleasant. *Name given when it is perceived that the birth of a child will make the home more pleasant.* (NGUNI)

Mncedisi Mncedi Helper. (NGUNI)

Mndeni Family or descendants. (NGUNI)

Mndenimunye We are one family. (NGUNI)

Mndeniwandile The family has increased. (NGUNI)

Mnewethu (m) My kinsmen. (NGUNI)

Mngeteli (m) One who has added to the number of the children in the family. (XITSONGA)

Mnikazi (m) The owner. (NGUNI)

Mnikel (m) One who gives generously. (NGUNI)

Mnikezonke (m) Give them all their due. *The child naming was a chance for the mother to put pressure on the father to finish paying the 'lobola' balance.* (NGUNI)

Mninaawa (m) The younger brother. (NGUNI)

Mninwa (m) Narrow. (NGUNI)

Mnqandeni (m) You must stop him/correct him. (NGUNI)

Mnqobi (m) The one who conquers. (NGUNI)

Mnqophiso (m) An agreement. (NGUNI)

Mnqwelo (m) Desire. *This name expresses the parents' relief when their desire for a child has been granted.* (NGUNI)

Mnqwenekile Desired. *This name expresses the parents' relief when their desire for a child has been granted.* (NGUNI)

Mntakama My mother's child. (NGUNI)

Mntanakhe His child. *This name is associated with paternity.* (NGUNI)

Mntanam My child. (NGUNI)

Mntanenkosi The child belongs to the royal family. (NGUNI)

Mntanomhle (m) The king. (NGUNI)

Mntfwana Literally 'small person', meaning 'child'. (NGUNI)

Mntomuhle A beautiful person. (NGUNI)

Mnukwa The suspect. *The name-giver wanted to level an allegation through this name.* (NGUNI)

Mnyamana Dark-skinned child. (NGUNI)

Mnyamezeli One who perseveres. (NGUNI)

Mnzondeni (m) Hate him. *Protective name used to shield the child against evil intentions/spirits.* (NGUNI)

Moagi (m) Builder; a citizen. (SOTHO)

Moahlodi (m) Judge. (SOTHO)

Moakgofi (m) One who hastens. *The child was born prematurely.* (SOTHO)

Moalafi (m) One who heals. *Name that depicts the name-giver's trade or talents.* (SOTHO)

Moanegi (m) Storyteller. (SOTHO)

Moapesi (m) One who covers. (SOTHO)

Moarabi (m) One who answers. *This is in reference to God.* (SOTHO)

Moatisi (m) Help us to increase. (SOTHO)

Moato (f) Increase. (SOTHO)

Mobotse (f) Beautiful. (SOTHO)

Modi (f) Short form of 'Modiegi'. (SOTHO)

Modiegi (f) The slow or delayed one. (SOTHO)

Modikadiki (f) One who hesitates. (SOTHO)

Modilana (m) Circumcised youth. (SOTHO)

Modirakhutso (m) Peacemaker. (SOTHO)

Modise (m) Herdboy. (SOTHO)

Modisha (m) Shepherd. (SOTHO)

Modjaji Rain Queen. (SOTHO)

Modupe Child born during a drizzle. (SOTHO)

Moeketsi The multiplier; proliferator. (SOTHO)

Moeletsi Advisor. (SOTHO)

Moeng A guest; a visitor. (SOTHO)

Moetapele Leader; captain. (SOTHO)

Mofedi One who feeds others. (SOTHO)

Mofelegetsi One who accompanies. (SOTHO)

Mofenyi Conqueror. (SOTHO)

Moferefere Confusion; conflict. (SOTHO)

Mofetodi One who replies. (SOTHO)

Mofosi One who misses the mark. (SOTHO)

Mogageso One of our own people. (SOTHO)

Mogale Courageous and witty one. *Reflecting physical and mental strength.* (SOTHO)

Mogami The one who milks (cows and goats). (SOTHO)

Moganedi **Mogani** One who refuses. (SOTHO)

Mogapi One who confiscates. (SOTHO)

Mogatsaka (f) Wife. (SOTHO)

Mogomotsi (m) One who brings me comfort. (SOTHO)

Mogorosi (m) One who brings the animals into the kraal in the evening. (SOTHO)

Mogotsi (m) The igniter of fire. (SOTHO)

Mohapi (m) Victor. (SOTHO)

Mohato (m) Step. *As in, a step towards something.* (SOTHO)

Mohau (m) Pity; mercy. (SOTHO)

Mohlabanedi (m) One who defends. (SOTHO)

Mohlabani (m) Soldier; warrior. (SOTHO)

Mohlahli (m) Leader; guide. (SOTHO)

Mohlalefi (m) A wise person. (SOTHO)

Mohlalosi (m) One who explains. (SOTHO)

Mohloalwa (m) The hated one. (SOTHO)

Mohlodi (m) Conqueror. (SOTHO)

Mohlokomedi (m) One who takes care. (SOTHO)

Mohlomi (m) The founder or the planter. (SOTHO)

Mohlomphegi (m) Honourable one. (SOTHO)

Mohlomphi (m) One who respects. (SOTHO)

Mohumi (m) The rich one. (SOTHO)

Mohunolodi (m) Liberator. (SOTHO)

Mohuta (m) Kind; type; sort. (SOTHO)

Moifa (m) Be afraid of him. (SOTHO)

Moipone (m) Self-admirer. (SOTHO)

Mojalefa (m) Heir. (SOTHO)

Mokga (m) Kind; sort; species. (SOTHO)

Mokgadi (m) Counsellor. (SOTHO)

Mokgethi (m) Chooser; one who will choose. (SOTHO)

Mokgosi (m) A loud call for help. (SOTHO)

Mokhasi (m) Crawler. (SOTHO)

Mokhethi (m) Chooser; one who will choose. (SOTHO)

Mokoto (m) A thing of naught. *Protective name given to child born after successive infant deaths.* (SOTHO)

Molamo (m) Brother-in-law. (SOTHO)

Molapo (m) Stream; river. *Name of former Sotho Chief.* (SOTHO)

Molatelo (m) Follower. (SOTHO)

Molatlhegi (m) The lost one. (SOTHO)

Molebogeng (m) Gratitude. (SOTHO)

Moleboheng (m) Gratitude for the birth. (SOTHO)

Molefe Molefi (m) One who pays damages to another. (SOTHO)

Molelekeng (f) Disown; sack her. (SOTHO)

Moleofi (m) A sinner. (SOTHO)

Moloki (m) Righteous one. (SOTHO)

Moloko He / She has good manners. (SOTHO)

Molokolli One who sets free. (SOTHO)

Molome (m) Uncle. (SOTHO)

Molopolodi (m) Redeemer. (SOTHO)

Molwantwa He/She fights the battle. (SOTHO)

Momelezi The one who strengthens and consolidates. (NGUNI)

Mompati One who accompanies me. (SOTHO)

Mona Wickedness. (XITSONGA)

Monaheng (m) One of the ancestral chiefs. (SOTHO)

Monareng (m) From the word 'linare': meaning Buffaloes. *This name represents fierceness of spirit.* (SOTHO)

Mondli (m) The one who rears and brings up. (NGUNI)

Mondlikazi (f) Foster mother. (NGUNI)

Money (m) Owner; master; lord. (SOTHO)

Mong (m) Lord. (SOTHO)

Mongameli (m) Overseer. (NGUNI)

Mongezi (m) One who adds. (NGUNI)

Moniwa (f) One who has been defaulted or sinned against. *This name can be given when the mother was raped or suffered a teenage pregnancy.* (NGUNI)

Monomolele (m) Liberator. (SOTHO)

Monosi (m) The only child in the family. (SOTHO)

Monwabisi (m) One who brings rejoicing. (NGUNI)

Mooketsi (m) One who increases. (SOTHO)

Mookho (m) Tear; lacrimation. (SOTHO)

Mophethi (m) One who has accomplished. (SOTHO)

Mophomodi (m) One who rests. (SOTHO)

Mophomotsi (m) Giver of rest. (SOTHO)

Mophudi (m) One who opens up. *Can be given to a first born who opens the womb.* (SOTHO)

Moputso (m) Reward. (SOTHO)

Morapedi (m) A prayerful man. (SOTHO)

Moratuoa Moratuwa Darling. (SOTHO)

Moremi (m) One who cuts with an axe; woodcutter. (SOTHO)

Moreri (m) One who is a preacher. (SOTHO)

Morero (m) Purpose. (SOTHO)

Morongwa (f) Angel. *Name given for the only girl in the family.* (SOTHO)

Morui (m) Rich one. (SOTHO)

Morutabana (f) Teacher; governess. (SOTHO)

Morutiši Teacher. (SOTHO)

Morwa (m) Our son. (SOTHO)

Mosa Grace. (SOTHO)

Mosadi (f) Wife. *This name is reserved for a married woman who has given birth.* (SOTHO)

Mosebetsi (m) Worker. (SOTHO)

Mosego Laughter. (SOTHO)

Mosegofatswa Blessed one. (SOTHO)

Mosek One who appears before a court. *The child may have been born when there was a court dispute in a family.* (SOTHO)

Mosela (m) The last one. (SOTHO)

Moselantja (m) Dog's tail. *Protective name given to shield the child against evil intentions/spirits.* (SOTHO)

Mosemodi (m) Traditional boy's name from legends. (SOTHO)

Mosemotsane (f) Diminutive form of 'Mosemodi'. *Both are used often with twins.* (SOTHO)

Mosetsana (f) Girl. (SOTHO)

Mosetsanagape (f) It's a girl again. (SOTHO)

Moshemane Moshanyana (m) Boy. (SOTHO)

Moshoeshoe (m) Flower. *From the tsikitlane plant. Also, first name of former Sotho king, who was a notable leader.* (SOTHO)

Mosidi (m) Grinder. (SOTHO)

Mosimane (m) Boy. (SOTHO)

Mosimanegape (m) It's a boy again. (SOTHO)

Mosimodi Mosimoli (m) Traditional fable name. (SOTHO)

Mosimotsana (m) *See 'Mosetsana'.*

Mosireletsi (m) Protector; defender; guardian. (SOTHO)

Mosupetsi (m) One who points out something to someone. (SOTHO)

Mosweu (m) The light-coloured one. (SOTHO)

Mothaetsi Obedient one. (SOTHO)

Mothakgalo Happiness. (SOTHO)

Motheo Foundation. *The mother rededicated her life to the Lord at the birth of the child.* (NGUNI)

Motheo Principle. (SOTHO)

Mothibi One who drives animals. (SOTHO)

Mothokgami Upright person. (SOTHO)

Mothusi One who helps. (SOTHO)

Motiisetsi One who perseveres. (SOTHO)

Motiisi One who strengthens. (SOTHO)

Motlale One who comes. (SOTHO)

Motlalentwa One who comes with war. (SOTHO)

Motlalepula The rain bringer. (SOTHO)

Motlamaganyi One who binds together. (SOTHO)

Motlamegi Guardian. (SOTHO)

Motlatsetsi Helper. (SOTHO)

Motle Beautiful. (SOTHO)

Motlhokomedi One in charge. (SOTHO)

Motlhophi One who chooses. (SOTHO)

Motli One who comes. (SOTHO)

Motlisi He who brings. (SOTHO)

Motlodiwa Anointed one. (SOTHO)

Motlogolo (m) Nephew. (SOTHO)

Motsamai (m) Traveller. (SOTHO)

Motseba (m) One who knows. (SOTHO)

Motshepegi (m) Trusted one. (SOTHO)

Motsotsi (m) One who rises up. (SOTHO)

Motsumi (m) The seeker; hunter. (SOTHO)

Moyahabo (f) She is getting married to her relative. *The name tells the story of what was going on at the time.* (SOTHO)

Moyisi (m) Victor. (NGUNI)

Mpatho (m) Care. *This name is advice to the mother to take good care, not only of the child, but also of her marital home.* (NGUNI)

Mpati (m) Ruler. (NGUNI)

Mpazamo (m) An error. *Name usually given after an unplanned pregnancy.* (NGUNI)

Mpendulo Mpendu (m) Answer. (NGUNI)

Mpfareleli Mpfari (m) Asking for forgiveness. (TSHIVENDA)

Mpfuleni (m) In the rain. *Name given to one born on a rainy day.* (XITSONGA)

Mpfuxi (m) One who encourages others. (XITSONGA)

Mphafane (m) Praiser. (SOTHO)

Mphakamisi (m) One who raises. (NGUNI)

Mphakati (m) Councillor. (XITSONGA)

Mphangeli (m) One who outruns the others. (NGUNI)

Mphathi (m) One who governs. (NGUNI)

Mphedisa (m) Help me to live. (SOTHO)

Mphedziseni (m) Finish me off. *Protective name given to shield the bearer from evil intentions/spirits.* (TSHIVENDA)

Mphikeleli (m) **Maphikelela** (m) Persistent; persevering. (NGUNI)

Mphikeni (m) Deny him. *Usually given when the father has denied that the child is his.* (NGUNI)

Mphikwa (m) The denied one. *Usually given when the father has denied that the child is his.* (NGUNI)

Mphinhlanhla (m) Given fortune. (NGUNI)

Mpho A present; gift. (SOTHO)

Mphokuhle Given a good thing. (NGUNI)

Mphumzi One who relieves. (NGUNI)

Mphuphi (m) A dreamer. (NGUNI)

Mphuthumi (m) The one who hastens. (NGUNI)

Mpikeleli (m) The ever-diligent one. (NGUNI)

Mpiliso One who has been made to recover. (NGUNI)

Mpilo Health. (NGUNI)

Mpilonhle Wishes for a good and healthy life. (NGUNI)

Mpindzulo Benefit. (XITSONGA)

Mpinkulu (m) Big battle. (NGUNI)

Mpisendlini (m) The war is within the house. (NGUNI)

Mpiyakhe (m) It is his battle. (NGUNI)

Mpogwanyana (m) The little noise. (XITSONGA)

Mpolayeng (m) Kill me. *This is a protective name given in order to shield the child from evil intentions/spirits.* (SOTHO)

Mponeng (m) Look at me. (SOTHO)

Mpumelelo Mpume Success. (NGUNI)

Mqhelewenkosi (m) The Lord's crown. (NGUNI)

Mqhubi (m) One who urges on. (NGUNI)

Mqo (m) Short form of 'Mqokeleli'. (NGUNI)

Mqokeleli (m) One who gathers. (NGUNI)

Mqolora (m) Self-willed one. (NGUNI)

Mqondisi (m) One who directs. (NGUNI)

Msakayise (m) The son of his father. (NGUNI)

Msalela (m) One who trails behind. (NGUNI)

Msanyana (m) Small boy. (NGUNI)

Msawenkosi (m) God's abundant grace. (NGUNI)

Mseni (m) One with grace. (NGUNI)

Mshana My sister's child. (NGUNI)

Mshayandlela (m) The striker of the road. *Traditional folktale name.* (NGUNI)

Mshosholozi (m) Rapid mover. *Also given to railway trains.* (NGUNI)

Msila (m) Literally meaning 'tail'. *Name given to a chief's messenger who carries a white ox tail.* (NGUNI)

Msimelelo (m) The one we lean on. (NGUNI)

Msimisi (m) The one who brings stability. (NGUNI)

Msiti Msizi (m) Helper. (NGUNI)

Msolanto (m) He is distrustful about this thing. *Names like this can be given as a paternity accusation.* (NGUNI)

Msulwa (m) Innocent one. (NGUNI)

Msuthukazi (m) Of the Basotho. (NGUNI)

Mswelazonke (m) He who is in need of everything. (NGUNI)

Mtamo (m) An attempt. (NGUNI)

Mtfokotisi (m) One who makes happy. (NGUNI)

Mtfunti (m) Shelter. (NGUNI)

Mtha (m) Short form of 'Mthandeni'. (NGUNI)

Mthabisi (m) The one who brings joy. (NGUNI)

Mthaka (m) Short form of 'Mthakazeli'. (NGUNI)

Mthakazeli (m) One who chants clan praises. (NGUNI)

Mthandazo One obtained through prayer. (NGUNI)

Mthandeni (m) Love him. (NGUNI)

Mthembeni (m) Trust Him. (NGUNI)

Mthetheleli (m) The one who forgives. (NGUNI)

Mthetho (m) Law. (NGUNI)

Mthobeli (m) The obedient one. (NGUNI)

Mthokozisi (m) The one who brings happiness. (NGUNI)

Mtholephi (m) Where is this child from? *Sometimes this name may be given to a child whose mother was not engaged in any open relationship.* (NGUNI)

Mthophi (m) One who chants praises. (NGUNI)

Mthulisi (m) Comforter. *A child born soon after a death or tragedy may have this name.* (NGUNI)

Mthunywa (m) The sent one. (NGUNI)

Mthunzi (m) Shadow. (NGUNI)

Mthuthuzeli (m) The comforter. *A child born soon after a death or tragedy may have this name.* (NGUNI)

Mtjhana (m) Nephew. (SOTHO)

Mtlhangi (m) The sufferer. *The family suffered some misfortune around the time of the mother's pregnancy.* (NGUNI)

Mtoti (f) Sweet. (NGUNI)

Mtsalane (f) Eye-catching one. (NGUNI)

Mtsetfo (m) Law. (NGUNI)

Mtshakazi (f) A young bride. (NGUNI)

Muaki (m) Builder. *A child is said to build a home.* (XITSONGA)

Mualusi (m) Guardian. (TSHIVENDA)

Muambiwa (m) One who is spoken of; famous one. (TSHIVENDA)

Muangelo The one to be sent; angel. (TSHIVENDA)

Mubasanyana See 'Mulungwanyana'. (XITSONGA)

Mubebi A parent. (TSHIVENDA)

Mubvana (f) Young married woman with one child. (TSHIVENDA)

Mudalo (m) Abundance. (TSHIVENDA)

Mudanagundo (m) The one who brought in victory. (TSHIVENDA)

Mudivhisi (m) An announcer. (TSHIVENDA)

Mudlayi (m) Murderer. (XITSONGA)

Muduma phansi (m) Thunder on earth. (XITSONGA)

Mudyondzisiwa (m) Disciple. (XITSONGA)

Muelelahukhethwa (m) Pilgrim. (TSHIVENDA)

Mufana (m) Boy. (XITSONGA)

Mufanafutsi (m) It is a boy again. (NGUNI)

Mufarisi (m) A helper. (TSHIVENDA)

Mufhatisani (m) A neighbour. (TSHIVENDA)

Mufunwa A beloved one. (TSHIVENDA)

Mufunziwa Disciple. (TSHIVENDA)

Muhali A courageous person. (TSHIVENDA)

Muhatuli (m) A judge. (TSHIVENDA)

Muhlayisi (m) Preserver. (XITSONGA)

Muhle (f) See 'Zinhle'.

Muhluri Victor. (XITSONGA)

Muhumbeli An applicant. (TSHIVENDA)

Muhura A neighbour. (TSHIVENDA)

Muhwali One who carries a burden. (TSHIVENDA)

Muhweleli A plaintiff. (TSHIVENDA)

Muhwelelwa A defendant. (TSHIVENDA)

Muimbi A singer. (TSHIVENDA)

Muimeleli An advocate. (TSHIVENDA)

Muimeli Representative. (TSHIVENDA)

Muingameli An inspector. (TSHIVENDA)

Mukalaha (m) An old man. (TSHIVENDA)

Mukalanga A Shona person. (TSHIVENDA)

Mukaluli Zealot. (TSHIVENDA)

Mukegulu (f) An old woman. (TSHIVENDA)

Mukelwe One who has been welcomed. (NGUNI)

Mukene So-and-so. (TSHIVENDA)

Mukhethwa The chosen one. (TSHIVENDA)

Mukhuhlwana The one who coughs. *The father might have used coughing to assert his authority.* (XITSONGA)

Mukhwe (f) Wife's father. (NGUNI)

Mukokonono Name from the Mukokonono tree. *It is a very hard wood used to make handles.* (XITSONGA)

Mukololo A prince or princess. (TSHIVENDA)

Mukondeleli One who perseveres. (TSHIVENDA)

Mukutsiri Redeemer, liberator. (XITSONGA)

Mukutsuriwa Redeemed. (XITSONGA)

Mukwasha (m) Bridegroom. (TSHIVENDA)

Mulahleki The one who lost his way. *This name might be given to a child from an unwanted pregnancy.* (XITSONGA)

Mulaifa Heir. (TSHIVENDA)

Mulalo Peace. (TSHIVENDA)

Mulambilu One who worries too much. (TSHIVENDA)

Mulamu My in-law. (NGUNI)

Mulandzeti Follower. (XITSONGA)

Mulanguli Organiser. (TSHIVENDA)

Mulanguteri One who watches over you. (XITSONGA)

Mulayo Law. (TSHIVENDA)

Mulimisi (m) Farmer. (TSHIVENDA)

Mulinda (m) One who looks after. (TSHIVENDA)

Mulindathavha (m) One who looks after the mountain. *The child is regarded as the successor of the traditional leader of the village.* (TSHIVENDA)

Mulisa (m) Shepherd. (TSHIVENDA)

Mulungwanyana (f) The little fair one. (XITSONGA)

Mulweri (m) One who fights for. (XITSONGA)

Munene The good one. (XITSONGA)

Mungomanyana The little witch doctor. *The mother will give such a name to defy public opinions about her when people accuse her of witchcraft.* (XITSONGA)

Muntomuhle A beautiful person. (NGUNI)

Muntu A person. (NGUNI)

Muntukabani Whose are you? *The father had his doubts regarding the paternity of the child.* (NGUNI)

Muntukafi (m) Person who does not die. (NGUNI)

Muntukayise (m) The person who belongs to his father. (NGUNI)

Muntuza Little person. See *'Muntu'*. (NGUNI)

Munyama Dark-skinned child. (XITSONGA)

Munyumana The timid one. (XITSONGA)

Mupfumedzanyi Mediator. (TSHIVENDA)

Mupfuni Helper. (XITSONGA)

Muphosi (m) The grave digger. *The mother might have died giving birth to the name-bearer.* (XITSONGA)

Muponisi (m) Saviour. (XITSONGA)

Murendeni (m) Praise Him. *Name given to praise God for the gift of a child.* (TSHIVENDA)

Murerelo Prayer. (TSHIVENDA)

Murhandziwa Beloved. (XITSONGA)

Murhangeli (m) Leader. (XITSONGA)

Murunwa (f) The one to be sent; angel. *Mother had a number of boys and had been longing for a girl.* (TSHIVENDA)

Musa Grace. (NGUNI)

Musawenkosi God's grace. (NGUNI)

Musekene (m) One who is thin. *From the expression 'muthu musekene o uwa' meaning: a thin person has gone.* (TSHIVENDA)

Muselwa (f) The bride. (TSHIVENDA)

Mushavho (m) Great trek; run away. *It may also be used to refer to escaping from an abusive relationship/marriage.* (TSHIVENDA)

Mushimane (m) Boy. (SOTHO)

Mushoni (m) Shame them. *Meaning, shame the ones who did not wish the family well.* (TSHIVENDA)

Musiiwa (m) Left behind. (TSHIVENDA)

Musiwalwo (m) It is time. *This is an expression used when something is long overdue.* (TSHIVENDA)

Mutafela (m) Might also die. *Name expressing fear after the death of siblings.* (SOTHO)

Mutambi (m) Player. (TSHIVENDA)

Mutanganedzi (m) Receiver. (TSHIVENDA)

Muthakhati (m) Witch. *A woman accused of witchcraft might give her child this name, thereby declaring that she defies public opinion.* (XITSONGA)

Muthu (m) A person. (TSHIVENDA)

Muthuhadini (m) One who is not troublesome. *Derived from an expression which states that a person is not troublesome but his deeds are.* (TSHIVENDA)

Muthuhathonwi (m)   A person is not provoked. *This type of personal name is used as a warning to people who undermine others, especially the quiet ones. A similar English idiomatic expression is 'Still waters runs deep'.*
(TSHIVENDA)

Muthundinne (m)   I am the person. (TSHIVENDA)

Muthundinnyi (m)   Who is the person? (TSHIVENDA)

Muthuphei (m)   One who is suffering. *A chance for the name-giver to register a complaint.* (TSHIVENDA)

Mutimi (m)   The one who extinguishes the fire. *The birth of a child has calmed a tense situation at home.*
(XITSONGA)

Mutloanyana (m)   Little rabbit. (SOTHO)

Mutondi (f)   The care-giver. *This refers to God.*
(TSHIVENDA)

Mutsaki (f)   The happy one. (XITSONGA)

Mutsala-matimu (m)   A historian. (XITSONGA)

Mutsala-vutomi (m)   One who writes life; a biographer.
(XITSONGA)

Mutshembi (m)   The one who trusts. (XITSONGA)

Mutshena (m)   One who is light in complexion.
(TSHIVENDA)

Mutshidzi (m)   Saviour. (TSHIVENDA)

Mutshutshu   Mutshutshudzi   One who encourages or excites bad behaviour.

Mutshwuku (f) Of light complexion. (TSHIVENDA)

Mutsila (m) Artist. (TSHIVENDA)

Mutsundzuxi (m) The one who reminds. (XITSONGA)

Muvanyisi (m) The judge. (XITSONGA)

Muvhambadzi (m) Salesperson. (TSHIVENDA)

Muvhigo (m) Report. (TSHIVENDA)

Muvhuso (m) Government. *The name was given to a person born in 1979 when the then Republic of Venda received its independence from the Republic of South Africa.* (TSHIVENDA)

Muvhuye (f) Sister-in-law. (TSHIVENDA)

Muyimeri (m) Defender. (XITSONGA)

Muzamani (m) One who has attempted. (NGUNI)

Muzi (m) A home. (NGUNI)

Muzikawaliwa (m) The home will not be refused. (NGUNI)

Muzikawulahlwa (m) The home cannot be overthrown. (NGUNI)

Muzikawungcwatsha (m) The home will not be buried. (NGUNI)

Muzikayise (m) His father's home. (NGUNI)

Muziwakhe (m) His home. (NGUNI)

Muziwandile (m) Our home has increased. (NGUNI)

Muziwenduku (m) Home of the whip. *Name given because the father will use the stick to solve every family problem.* (NGUNI)

Muziwenkosi (m) The Lord's home. (NGUNI)

Muziwethu (m) Our home. (NGUNI)

Muziwoxolo (m) A peaceful home. (NGUNI)

Muzwokuthula (m) The home of peace. *Other than the literal meaning, this can be a warning to those who want to bring discord into the family that this is a peaceful home.* (NGUNI)

Muzwoxolo (m) The home of reconciliation. (NGUNI)

Mvangeli (m) The one who preaches good news. (NGUNI)

Mvano Co-operation. (NGUNI)

Mveku A little baby. (NGUNI)

Mvelaphanda Advancement. (TSHIVENDA)

Mvelelo Result. (TSHIVENDA)

Mvelo Nature. (NGUNI)

Mvuledzo Conclusion. *Name used for the last-born child.* (TSHIVENDA)

Mvuleni In the rain. *The child was born on a rainy day.* (NGUNI)

Mvusakufa (m) One who awakes what has been dead. *Name can be given when the child resembles a dead relation.* (NGUNI)

Mvuselelo (m) Revival. *Parents might give a name like this in the hope that this child will be the one who will revive their souls.* (NGUNI)

Mvuseni (m) Wake him up. (NGUNI)

Mvusi (m) One who awakes/arouses. (NGUNI)

Mvuyelwa (m) We are rejoicing at the birth of this child. (NGUNI)

Mvuyisi (m) One who brings joy. (NGUNI)

Mvuzi (m) A rewarder. (NGUNI)

Mvuzo A reward. (NGUNI)

Mwanhlanhla-Mukhamu The one who unties the girdle. *Meaning, the one who opens the womb. It is a name often given to a first-born child.* (XITSONGA)

Mwaxilenge (m) Daughter of the little leg. (XITSONGA)

Mwaxinengana (m) *See 'Mwaxilenge'.*

Mxokozeli (m) The noisy one. (NGUNI)

Mxoleli (m) One who easily forgives. (NGUNI)

Mxolisi (m) The one bringing forgiveness instead of condemnation. (NGUNI)

Mzabalazo (m) *See 'Zabalazile'.*

Mzwakhe (m) His own homestead. (NGUNI)

Mzala My cousin. (NGUNI)

Mzali A parent. (NGUNI)

Mzalwane Near kinsman; brethren. (NGUNI)

Mzamo Trial. (NGUNI)

Mzamomuhle A good trial. (NGUNI)

Mzangoba Hear by hearsay. (SOTHO)

Mzansi Mzantsi South. (NGUNI)

Mzi (m) Short form of 'Mziwethu, Mzikayise'. (NGUNI)

Mzikawupheli (m) The family line will not end. (NGUNI)

Mzikayise (m) Father's household. *A combination of 'Muzi' and 'Uyise'.* (NGUNI)

Mzikazi (m) Big household. (NGUNI)

Mzikiziki (m) Single and unaided person. (NGUNI)

Mzilikazi (m) A pathway. (NGUNI)

Mzimasi (m) We are now supported. (NGUNI)

Mziwethu (m) Our home. *A combination of 'Umuzi' and 'Owethu'.* (NGUNI)

Mziwoxolo (m) Peaceful home. *A combination of 'Umuzi' and 'Uxolo'.* (NGUNI)

Mziyanda (m) Our household has increased. *A combination of 'Umuzi' and 'Uyanda'.* (NGUNI)

Mzo (m) Short form of 'Mzoxolo' or 'Mzolisi'. (NGUNI)

Mzodumo (m) Noble and famous household. *A combination 'Umuzi' and 'Udumo'.* (NGUNI)

Mzoli (m) A short form of 'Mzolisi'. (NGUNI)

Mzolisi (m) A man of peace and tranquility. (NGUNI)

Mzomuhle (m) A beautiful home. (NGUNI)

Mzonjani (m) What kind of a home is this? *Usually said when relations do not get along.* (NGUNI)

Mzontsundu (m) African family. (NGUNI)

Mzonzima (m) The troubled home. (NGUNI)

Mzoxolo (m) *See 'Mziwoxolo'.*

Mzu (m) Short form of 'Mzukisi'. (NGUNI)

Mzukisi (m) Make famous. (NGUNI)

Mzukulu My grandchild. (NGUNI)

Mzuvukile (m) The one who will rebuild our home. *A combination of 'Umuzi' and 'Uvukile'.* (NGUNI)

Mzwa (m) Short form of 'Mzwandile'. (NGUNI)

Mzwakhe (m) His household. (NGUNI)

Mzwandile (m) The family has increased. (NGUNI)

Mzwanele (m) The home is now complete. (NGUNI)

Mzwawamadoda (m) Male-dominated home. (NGUNI)

Mzweleni (m) Have mercy on him. (NGUNI)

Mzwenhlanhla (m) Home of fortune. *This name can be given when everything seems to go as wished for.* (NGUNI)

Mzwilili (f) Canary. *One with a beautiful voice.* (NGUNI)

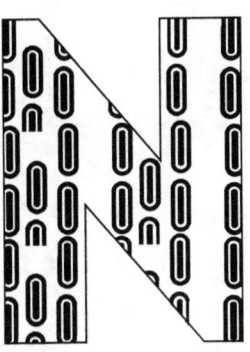

Naba (f) Here they are. (NGUNI)

Naba (f) Stretch. (SOTHO)

Nabongwe (f) Daughter of the 'Mahlangu' clan. (NGUNI)

Naka (f) Beautiful. (TSHIVENDA)

Nakaho (f) Attractive. (TSHIVENDA)

Naki (f) Care. (TSHIVENDA)

Nakisa (f) Beautify. (TSHIVENDA)

Nakisani (f) Make it beautiful. (TSHIVENDA)

Nakiwe (f) One who gets attention. (NGUNI)

Nala (f) The prosperous one. (NGUNI)

Naledi (f) Star. (SOTHO)

Naledzani Nale (f) When someone refuses to take back something that belongs to them after it has been taken away. *This is a protective name given to shield the child from misfortune.* (TSHIVENDA)

Naledzi (f) Star. (TSHIVENDA)

Naleli (f) Star. (SOTHO)

Namadzavho Your meat. *Telling the messenger of death 'Here is your meat'. This would occur if there have been several deaths preceding this child's birth.* (TSHIVENDA)

Nambita (f) Taste. (NGUNI)

Nambyeni In the river. *Name based on the place of birth.* (XITSONGA)

Namhla (f) Today. *Marking a special day.* (NGUNI)

Namile (f) The excited one. (NGUNI)

Namisile (f) Bringer of happiness. (NGUNI)

Namkoneni (f) Daughter of the 'Masombuka' clan. (NGUNI)

Namotse (f) Helped; rescued; intervened. (SOTHO)

Nana (f) Infant. (SOTHO)

Nandala (f) Daughter of the 'Mtsweni' clan. (NGUNI)

Nande (f) Short form of 'Nandipha'. (NGUNI)

Nandi (f) The sweet one. *The first name of the mother of 19th century Zulu warrior king Shaka Zulu.* (NGUNI)

Nandipa (f) We have been gifted. (NGUNI)

Nandipha (f) We have been given. (NGUNI)

Nandisa (f) One who sweetens. *The birth of a child may be looked upon as a hope to bring sweetness in a marital relationship.* (NGUNI)

Nandisile (f) One who has sweetened. (NGUNI)

Nandiswa (f) Sugary and lovable. (NGUNI)

Nanga (f) Choose. (TSHIVENDA)

Nangamso (f) Do the same tomorrow. *The name is part of the expression 'ungadinwa nangomso'. It is used to show gratitude and to secure the same favour next time* (NGUNI)

Nangu (f) Here. (NGUNI)

Nangweto (f) Again; once more. (XITSONGA)

Nantobela (f) Daughter of the 'Mhlangu' clan. (NGUNI)

Nantsika What is the name? *When trying to recall someone's name.* (NGUNI)

Nare (m)   Buffalo. *Name given to someone who comes from the Leribe district in Lesotho.* (SOTHO)

Natha   Shine; be shiny. (SOTHO)

Nathi (m)   With us. *Name usually used as a short form of 'Nkosinathi'.* (NGUNI)

Nathivulo (m)   First boy. (XITSONGA)

Natlafala (m)   Become strong. (SOTHO)

Natlharini (f)   Daughter of the 'Skhosana' clan. (NGUNI)

Navalati (f)   Stretch out your legs and be at ease. (XITSONGA)

Nazo (f)   There they are. (NGUNI)

Nazulu (f)   Born on a rainy day. (NGUNI)

Ncamile (f)   Has been satisfied. *The parents' desire for another child or for a girl has been satisfied.* (NGUNI)

Ncamisa (f)   Cause the other to give up. *Such a name can be used in competitive situations, especially among the co-wives in a polygamous home.* (NGUNI)

Ncamisile (f)   Fulfilled, exceeding. (NGUNI)

Ncamiso (f)   Satisfaction. (NGUNI)

Ncane (f)   Small one. *Name given when the baby was smaller than expected.* (NGUNI)

Nceba (f)   Mercy. (NGUNI)

Ncebakazi (f)   See 'Nonceba'.

Nceda Ncedana (m) You must help; help each other. *This name reflects a general belief that an African child is the child of the community.* (NGUNI)

Ncedisa Ncediswa (f) Helper, the helped one. *This name reflects a general belief that an African child is the child of the community.* (NGUNI)

Ncediwe (f) The one who has been helped. (NGUNI)

Ncedo (m) Our helper. (NGUNI)

Nceku (m) One who supports and serves. (NGUNI)

Ncekukazi (f) A woman who serves and supports. (NGUNI)

Ncelebana (m) Spy. (NGUNI)

Ncengimpilo Struggling to survive. *Such a name may be given when a relative in the family is ill.* (NGUNI)

Ncengiwe (f) We have pleaded with her. *Marriages within the Nguni tribe were sometimes an arrangement between families rather than individuals; names such as this may reflect that the mother had initially refused to marry the husband chosen for her.* (NGUNI)

Ncila-wa-havu (m) Someone who moves everywhere, like the tail of the monkey. (XITSONGA)

Ncindzana (m) The little wild cat. *The tendency to use animal names is due to the behaviour, personality and certain character traits which the name-bearer is thought to share with a specific animal.* (XITSONGA)

Ncinyane (f) A little one. *Based on the physical appearance of the baby.* (NGUNI)

Ncobile Has conquered. (NGUNI)

Ncomekile Praiseworthy. (NGUNI)

Ncumisa (f) The one who brings a smile, melting our hearts. (NGUNI)

Ncumisile (f) One who has delighted us. (NGUNI)

Ncundzu Palm tree. *This name is from a riddle about the branches of the palm tree, which sweep the ground far away from the stem, leaving high grass and rubbish. It refers to a person who shows more kindness to strangers than to his relations.* (XITSONGA)

Ncunyiswa (f) Delighted. (NGUNI)

Ndaba (m) Story. *Name given to a famous person.* (NGUNI)

Ndabeni (m) Of the news. *Usually said of someone who always has a story to tell.* (NGUNI)

Ndabezinhle (m) Good news! (NGUNI)

Ndabezintsa (m) Fresh news. (NGUNI)

Ndabezitha (m) A clan praise name for a member of the Zulu family. *It is also used to honour the Zulu King.* (NGUNI)

Ndafika I have arrived. (NGUNI)

Ndanduleni Give me rest. (TSHIVENDA)

Ndanga Short form of 'Nndanganeni'. (TSHIVENDA)

Ndeko One who is a necessity. *The name is given to a child born to a previously childless couple.* (NGUNI)

Ndemedzo Ndeme A burden. (TSHIVENDA)

Ndidomushumela I will work for Him. (TSHIVENDA)

Ndidzulafhi (m) Where do I stay? *This personal name usually refers to a situation where there is no peace between members of the family, especially between the in-laws and the bride.* (TSHIVENDA)

Ndifhedzo (m) Revenge. *Name given with the hope that the holder will serve revenge for those responsible for evil against the family.* (TSHIVENDA)

Ndifho (m) Compensation. (TSHIVENDA)

Ndiitwani (m) What are you doing to me? (TSHIVENDA)

Ndikho (m) I am here. *Name given to a child who made a surprise entry, either through premature birth or despite the doctor's report that the child would not make it.* (NGUNI)

Ndileka (f) The dignified woman. (NGUNI)

Ndingasithebeni (m) The one who has no place to settle down. (NGUNI)

Ndingatshilidzi It is through the mercy of God. (TSHIVENDA)

Ndingedzo An attempt. (TSHIVENDA)

Ndiphiwe We have been given. (NGUNI)

Nditsheni Leave me. (TSHIVENDA)

Ndivheo Recognition. (TSHIVENDA)

Ndivhoniswani What am I shown? *The name-giver is amazed at the way the in-laws are treating her.* (TSHIVENDA)

Ndivhudza Ndivhu Ndivhudzannyi Who do I tell? *This name is found where the name-giver is complaining that she/he has been quiet for some time about ill-treatment.* (TSHIVENDA)

Ndivhuwo Ndivhuho I am grateful. *Name given by the paternal aunt encouraging the family to be thankful, despite the difficult circumstances they are facing.* (TSHIVENDA)

Ndivuyeleni Rejoice for me. (NGUNI)

Ndivuyiseni Rejoice with me. (NGUNI)

Ndiyafhi Where do I go? (TSHIVENDA)

Ndjombo Happiness. (XITSONGA)

Ndlala One who is hungry. (NGUNI)

Ndlebezikhanyilanga (m) The sun shines through the ears. *Zulu name for a fair-skinned person.* (NGUNI)

Ndlela (m) Of the way. *Name of Dingane's army commander who was killed by Dingane.* (NGUNI)

Ndlelenhle (f) Have a safe journey. *Name usually given to girls as they enter another stage of growth. The name is wishing them success.* (NGUNI)

Ndleleni On the way. *Name based on the place where the mother gave birth.* (NGUNI)

Ndleve Ear. (XITSONGA)

Ndlopfana (m) The little elephant. *The tendency to use animal names is due to the behaviour, personality and certain character traits which the name-bearer is thought to share with a specific animal.* (XITSONGA)

Ndlunkulu Of royalty. *This name is reserved only for Zulu royals.* (NGUNI)

Ndofa Loving one to death. (NGUNI)

Ndofela I will die where they die. *It is a pledge name for the dearly beloved.* (NGUNI)

Ndofhiwa I am given. (TSHIVENDA)

Ndongela One weak and lacking in vigour. (NGUNI)

Ndovhololo Repetition. (TSHIVENDA)

Nduma Rumours. (XITSONGA)

Ndumi Short form of 'Ndumiso'. (NGUNI)

Ndumiso Praise. (NGUNI)

Ndunduzo The comfort. (NGUNI)

Nduvho Giving praise. (TSHIVENDA)

Ndwebi (m) Timid, nervous and suspicious one. (NGUNI)

Ndzalama (m) Plenty of. *This name is taken from the noun 'ndzala' which signifies plenty.* (XITSONGA)

Ndzhakandzhaka (m) Heritage. (XITSONGA)

Ndzhopheni (m) In the mud. (XITSONGA)

Ndzindza n'waka (f) One who awaits the season. *Name given to a spinster.* (XITSONGA)

Ndzindza (m) Wait. (NGUNI)

Ndzivalelo (m) Forgiveness. (XITSONGA)

Ndzuzo (m) Gain. (NGUNI)

Neelo (m) Given. (SOTHO)

Nefefe (m) Royal name for the leader or owner of the place called Fefe. (TSHIVENDA)

Nelani (f) Be satisfied. (NGUNI)

Nele (f) Filled. (NGUNI)

Neledzi (f) Star. (TSHIVENDA)

Nelephi (f) Where can she be fulfilled? *Question-type names are usually associated with a mystery in the family surrounding the birth.* (NGUNI)

Neli (f) Short form of 'Neliswa', 'Nelisiwe'. (NGUNI)

Nelisa (f) *See 'Nelisiwe'.*

Nelisile (f) She has satisfied us. (NGUNI)

Nelisiwe Neliswa (f) Satisfied. (NGUNI)

Nematei (m) Medical specialist. (TSHIVENDA)

Nenekazi (f) A lady. (NGUNI)

Nenungwi (m) Royal name for the leader or owner of the place called Nenungwi. (TSHIVENDA)

Neo Gift; talent. (SOTHO)

Nêpô Precision. (SOTHO)

Nesiphiwo You are talented. (NGUNI)

Netshimbupfe (m) Royal name for the leader or owner of the place called Tshimbupfe. (TSHIVENDA)

Netulusani Bring refreshment. (TSHIVENDA)

Newô Gift; talent; present. (SOTHO)

Nezelela Nezela (f) Add another one (child). (NGUNI)

Nezile Nezelile (f) Has added upon. (NGUNI)

Nezipho (f) Gifted child. (NGUNI)

Neziswa Nezisa (f) One who brings satisfaction. (NGUNI)

Neziwe (f) She has been added. (NGUNI)

Ngam Through me. *Name given to express how proud the mother may feel about bringing the child into the world.* (NGUNI)

Ngamini By what/how? *This personal name reflects a situation where people are surprised by events.* (TSHIVENDA)

Ngani With what? *This personal name reflects a situation where people are surprised by events.* (NGUNI)

Ngathi Through us. *Their union has brought the child into the world.* (NGUNI)

Ngawethu They (the child) are ours. (NGUNI)

Ngcebo Wealth. (NGUNI)

Ngceboyakhe His wealth. (NGUNI)

Ngceboyami My wealth. (NGUNI)

Ngceboyethu Our wealth. (NGUNI)

Ngcwenti (m) An expert. (NGUNI)

Ngekengithule (m) I will not be quiet. *The name-giver is using the name to protest about their situation.* (NGUNI)

Ngenzeni What have I done? *The name-giver might have been ill-treated; through the name she wants answers for her suffering.* (NGUNI)

Ngesihle With goodness. (NGUNI)

Ngetela Addition to the family. (XITSONGA)

Nghunghunyana (m) *The name of the Shangaan's best-loved leader and their last true chief.*

Nghwendzha (m) Bachelor. (XITSONGA)

Ngibongiseni Help me to thank God. (NGUNI)

Ngiphile I have given. (NGUNI)

Ngoako House. (SOTHO)

Ngoana *Literally 'child' but also used by young men referring to girls.* (SOTHO)

Ngomana The little drum. (XITSONGA)

Ngomusa With grace. (NGUNI)

Ngonde The old and good one. (XITSONGA)

Ngongomela Evening star. (XITSONGA)

Ngqinisa Testify firmly. (NGUNI)

Ngqiqo One who is well thought of. (NGUNI)

Ngqondi An intelligent one. (NGUNI)

Ngqondongqondo The wise one. (NGUNI)

Ngqungqumbane Active and restless little one. (NGUNI)

Ngqwelengqwele (m) The champion. (NGUNI)

Ngununu (m) The huge one. (XITSONGA)

Ngwako (m) House; courtyard. *Child born after a number of infant deaths in the family. The name indicates that she must not be touched by outsiders.* (SOTHO)

Ngwanadikgale (m) Child of Dikgale family. (SOTHO)

Ngwanakutswa (m) Illegitimate child. (SOTHO)

Ngwanamoganong (f) The child of Mogonong family. (SOTHO)

Ngwanamogodi (f) The child of Mogodi family. (SOTHO)

Ngwanamolepo (f) The child of Molepo family. (SOTHO)

Ngwanamothiba (f) The child of Mothiba family. (SOTHO)

Ngwanana (f) Girl. (SOTHO)

Ngwanatladi (f) The child of Tladi family. (SOTHO)

Ngwanenyana (f) Small daughter. (SOTHO)

Ngwaneswane (f) Beloved one. (SOTHO)

Ngwanongwako (m) Child of the house. *Child born after a number of infant deaths in the family. The name indicates that she must not be touched by outsiders.* (SOTHO)

Ngwenya (m) The crocodile. *This name is now hardly used as a first name, but is common as a surname.* (TSONGA) (NGUNI)

Ngwili Great number of children in a family. (NGUNI)

Nhenha Hero. (XITSONGA)

Nhlabutelo Revelation. (XITSONGA)

Nhlakanipho Nhlaka The wise one. (NGUNI)

Nhlalala A bird. *Usually this bird tells a story or will give a warning when there is a snake in the vicinity.* (XITSONGA)

Nhlamulo Answer; reply. (XITSONGA)

Nhlanga Sign or mark. (XITSONGA)

Nhlanganiso An addition. (XITSONGA)

Nhlangolwani The exiled one. (XITSONGA)

Nhlanhla Luck. (NGUNI)

Nhlanhlayakhe His/her luck. (NGUNI)

Nhlanhlayethu Our luck. (NGUNI)

Nhlanzeko Purity. (NGUNI)

Nhlaselo Pursuit. (XITSONGA)

Nhlayisi The guardian. (XITSONGA)

Nhlego (f) Gift. (XITSONGA)

Nhliziyo (m) Friend of the heart. (NGUNI)

Nhlomulo (m) Sorrow. (XITSONGA)

Nhongana (m) The little stick. (XITSONGA)

Nibidyala New Year's Day's child. (NGUNI)

Nike Short form of 'Nikeziwe'. (NGUNI)

Nikelo Given. *Names such as this acknowledges the belief that children are a gift from God.* (NGUNI)

Nikelwa One who has been offered. (NGUNI)

Nikeziwe Given. *Names such as this acknowledges the belief that children are a gift from God.* (NGUNI)

Nikile Has given. (NGUNI)

Nikiwe Has been given. *Names such as this acknowledge the belief that children are a gift from God.* (NGUNI)

Niphile Have a long life. *This name is a blessing pronouncement.* (NGUNI)

Niphiwe You have been given. *Names such as this acknowledge the belief that children are a gift from God.* (NGUNI)

Njabulo Our joy. (NGUNI)

Njengele A brave and heroic one. (NGUNI)

Njengoyise He resembles his father. *The mother can name a child thus to answer some allegation concerning the paternity of the child.* (NGUNI)

Nkakamba (m) Tall, well-proportioned person. (XITSONGA)

Nkakatla (m) Very tall and strong person. (XITSONGA)

Nkaladyondziso (m) One lacking opportunity to learn. (XITSONGA)

Nkalakata (m) Strong young man of marriageable age. (XITSONGA)

Nkalamali (m) One who is lacking money. (XITSONGA)

Nkalamona (m) One who is patient. (XITSONGA)

Nkalampfuxelo (m) One without relations or friends. (XITSONGA)

Nkalanawulo (m) Have received their portion. (XITSONGA)

Nkalanga (m) Member of the Kalangas family. (XITSONGA)

Nkalavuyo (m) One without a home or friend. (XITSONGA)

Nkalaxaka (m) One with no relatives. (XITSONGA)

Nkantanga My darling. (XITSONGA)

Nkanyezi A star. (NGUNI)

Nkanyisi One who despises others. (XITSONGA)

Nkanyiso Light. (NGUNI)

Nkarabela Answer for me. (SOTHO)

Nkateko The lucky one. (XITSONGA)

Nkaxaka Illegitimate child. See *'Nkalaxaka'* (XITSONGA)

Nkaxivongo Illegitimate child. (XITSONGA)

Nkazana (f) A young married woman at her father's home. (NGUNI)

Nkazimulo Glorious one. (NGUNI)

Nkedama An orphan. (NGUNI)

Nkemisa Raise me. (SOTHO)

Nkgopotsa Remind me. *Usually used when the child is a constant reminder of circumstances surrounding the birth.* (SOTHO)

Nkhanedzeni (m) Disagree with me, or more accurately, disagree with me and face the consequences. (TSHIVENDA)

Nkhangweleni (m) Forgive me. *This name is a prayer to God, since the name-giver did not believe that she would be able to fall pregnant after a long time of childlessness.* (TSHIVENDA)

Nkhensani (f) Thanksgiving. (XITSONGA)

Nkhetheleng (f) Choose for me. (SOTHO)

Nkhinsamela (f) Adore. (XITSONGA)

Nkhomela (m) Pardon. (XITSONGA)

Nkhumbudzeni (m) Remind them. *Used usually when the child is a constant reminder of circumstances surrounding the birth.* (TSHIVENDA)

Nkhumbuleni (m) Remember me. (TSHIVENDA)

Nkinsimane (m) The wealthy man. (NGUNI)

Nkoe (m) Tiger. *The tendency to use animal names is due to the behaviour, personality and certain character traits which the name-bearer is thought to share with a specific animal.* (SOTHO)

Nkoenyane Nkoeneane (m) Little tiger. *The tendency to use animal names is due to the behaviour, personality and certain character traits which the name-bearer is thought to share with a specific animal.* (SOTHO)

Nkokone (m) Kinglet; little king. (XITSONGA)

Nkolo (m) Stubborn person. (XITSONGA)

Nkomokazikho (m) There are no cattle. *Meaning the father has not yet paid the 'lobola'.* (NGUNI)

Nkondzo (m) Foot; sole of the foot. (XITSONGA)

Nkosana (m) Prince; heir. (NGUNI)

Nkosazana (f) Princess. (NGUNI)

Nkosemntu (m) The human king. (NGUNI)

Nkosenhle (m) The good Lord. (NGUNI)

Nkosenye (m) One king; another king. (NGUNI)

Nkosi (m) King. (NGUNI)

Nkosi (m) Mourning. *Someone in the family might have died and the family was in mourning when the child was born.* (XITSONGA)

Nkosibonile The Lord has seen. *The father suspected that the child was not his, but decided to leave the matter in God's hands.* (NGUNI)

Nkosikhona The Lord is here. (NGUNI)

Nkosinamandla The Lord is powerful. (NGUNI)

Nkosinami God is with me. (NGUNI)

Nkosinathi God is with us. (NGUNI)

Nkosingiphile God has graciously given. *Names such as this acknowledge the belief that children are a gift from God.* (NGUNI)

Nkosinhle The King (i.e. God) is good. (NGUNI)

Nkosini What kind of king will he be? (NGUNI)

Nkosinomusa The Lord is kind/graceful. (NGUNI)

Nkosinothando God has love. (NGUNI)

Nkosiphendule The Lord has answered our prayer. (NGUNI)

Nkosiphile The Lord has given. *Names such as this acknowledge the belief that children are a gift from God.* (NGUNI)

Nkosisiphile The Lord has given unto us. *Names such as this acknowledge the belief that children are a gift from God.* (NGUNI)

Nkosithandile It has pleased the Lord. (NGUNI)

Nkosivumile (f) The Lord has allowed. (NGUNI)

Nkosiyabantu (m) King for the people. (NGUNI)

Nkoveni In the valley. *Name based on the place where the mother gave birth.* (XITSONGA)

Nkqubeko Progress. (NGUNI)

Nku (m) Sheep. *The tendency to use animal names is due to the behaviour, personality and certain character traits which the name-bearer is thought to share with a specific animal.* (SOTHO)

Nkululeko Liberty. *This may be a politically-inspired name.* (NGUNI)

Nkululo Release. *This may refer to the release from fear or from idle gossip regarding the mother's barrenness.* (NGUNI)

Nkunzana (m) The little bull. (TSONGA) (NGUNI)

Nkunzi (m) A bull. *Name used for a powerful or wealthy man.* (NGUNI)

Nkunzi-ku-nyanyuka (m) The fury or the great joy of the bull. (XITSONGA)

Nkure Short form of 'Nonkululeko'. (NGUNI)

Nkuthalo Active and industrious one. (NGUNI)

Nkwe (m) Tiger. *The tendency to use animal names is due to the behaviour, personality and certain character traits which the name-bearer is thought to share with a specific animal.* (SOTHO)

Nkwenyane (m) Little tiger. *The tendency to use animal names is due to the behaviour, personality and certain character traits which the name-bearer is thought to share with a specific animal.* (SOTHO)

Nkxentsi (f) A good dancer. (NGUNI)

Nndanganeni (m) A group of people planning to do something to someone. *The name-giver may use the name to expose a secret plot; usually employed within the chieftaincy homestead.* (TSHIVENDA)

Nndileni (m) Mourn me. *Given to protect the child against the evil eye.* (TSHIVENDA)

Nndini (m) Short form of 'Azwinndini'. (TSHIVENDA)

Nnditsheni (m) Leave me. *This personal name means that someone should be left alone, especially after having suffered torment at the hands of others.* (TSHIVENDA)

Nnduvheni (m) Pay homage to me. *Name given to royals, communicating to their subjects.* (TSHIVENDA)

Nndwakhulu (m) Big fight. *After a conflict in the family or community.* (TSHIVENDA)

Nndwamato (m) Eye fight. *When there is internal conflict and people are giving each other bad looks.* (TSHIVENDA)

Nndweleni (m) Fight for me. *This name is given to a headman who has been asked to assist the chief in looking after his subjects in another village.* (TSHIVENDA)

Nnete Nneteng Truth; verity. (SOTHO)

Nnyadzeni (m) Disrespect me. *Names such as this will be best interpreted as 'Disrespect me and you will see!' Most Venda names were originally given to the chiefs in order to communicate a message to their subjects, but these names have now filtered down to everyday use.* (TSHIVENDA)

Nnyaweleni Nnyawedzeni (m) Let me rest from suffering. *Name given to ask those around the name-giver to relieve her from suffering.* (TSHIVENDA)

Nobahlezi (f) The mother of Bahlezi. *When the woman is married she is usually referred to by the name of her child prefixed by No- .* (NGUNI)

Nobandla (f) One taking care of the family. *Name usually given to the new bride in her marital home.* (NGUNI)

Nobani (f) Such a one. (NGUNI)

Nobantu (f) Woman of the people. (NGUNI)

Nobanyazile (f) Look down upon. (NGUNI)

Nobathembu Nobatembu (f) She belongs to the family of 'Abathembu'. (NGUNI)

Nobhala (f) A writer; secretary. (NGUNI)

Nobhejile (f) She has gambled with her life. (NGUNI)

Nobubele (f) Compassionate one. (NGUNI)

Nobuhle (f) Beautiful daughter. (NGUNI)

Nobukhosi (f) Of royalty. (NGUNI)

Nobuntu (f) Mother of human kindness. (NGUNI)

Nobutho (f) Warrior. (NGUNI)

Nocanda (f) A surveyor. (NGUNI)

Nocawe (f) One born on Sunday. (NGUNI)

Nocingile (f) One who has been thought about. (NGUNI)

Nodinda (f) A very reserved one. (NGUNI)

Nodumo (f) Famous one. (NGUNI)

Nofanele (f) Suitable. (NGUNI)

Nofezile (f) She has accomplished. (NGUNI)

Nofikile (f) She has arrived. (NGUNI)

Nofungile (f) She has pledged. (NGUNI)

Nogqala (f) Of the Hottentots. (NGUNI)

Nohlobile (f) She has come to decorate our home. (NGUNI)

Nokhangela (f) One who looks on. (NGUNI)

Nokhanyiselo (f) *See 'Nokukhanya'.*

Nokhanyo (f) Daughter of the light. (NGUNI)

Nokhaya (f) Woman of a home. (NGUNI)

Nokhumbuzo (f) A woman who brings back the memories. (NGUNI)

Nokifisa (f) Desired daughter. (NGUNI)

Nokubonga (f) *See 'Abonga'.*

Nokuhle (f) One with goodness. (NGUNI)

Nokukhanya (f) Mother of light or enlightenment (i.e. wisdom). (NGUNI)

Nokulunga (f) *See 'Lunga'.*

Nokuphila (f) Mother of life. (NGUNI)

Nokuphiwa (f) Our given daughter. (NGUNI)

Nokusa (f) Daughter of the morning dawn. (NGUNI)

Nokuthula (f) Mother of quietness/peace. (NGUNI)

Nokuvela (f) Mother of nature. (NGUNI)

Nokuzola (f) Humbled one. (NGUNI)

Nokuzotha (f) Dignified one. (NGUNI)

Nokwakha (f) One building up the home. (NGUNI)

Nokwakhe (f) One with her belongings. (NGUNI)

Nokwanda (f) *See 'Ayanda'.*

Nokwayiyo (f) It is the girl. (NGUNI)

Nokwazi (f) The knowledgeable one. (NGUNI)

Nokwenama (f) Daughter of rejoicing. (NGUNI)

Nokwethemba (f) One with hope. (NGUNI)

Nokwezi (f) *See 'Nokhwezi'.*

Nolakhe (f) One who must build the home. *Name usually given to a bride in Xhosa culture with the hope that she will assist in building the homestead.* (NGUNI)

Nolita (f) Of the daylight. (NGUNI)

Nolitha (f) One who gives meaning to life. (NGUNI)

Nolithemba (f) Hope. (NGUNI)

Nolizwe (f) Daughter of the nation. (NGUNI)

Nolizwi (f) With a beautiful voice. (NGUNI)

Nolonwabiso (f) The cheerful one. (NGUNI)

Noloyiso (f) Victorious one. (NGUNI)

Nolubabalo (f) Mother of grace. (NGUNI)

Nolufefe (f) Mother of grace and modesty. (NGUNI)

Nolukhanyo (f) One who has brought the light. *See 'Khanyo'* (NGUNI)

Nolukholo (f) The believer. (NGUNI)

Nolumanyano (f) Unity. (NGUNI)

Nolumkile (f) You must be wise. (NGUNI)

Nolusindiso (f) God's salvation. (NGUNI)

Noluthando Nolutando (f) Love. (NGUNI)

Noluvo (f) One with an opinion. *This name was used by the mother in-law to address the assertive daughter in-law.* (NGUNI)

Noluvuyo (f) Mother of rejoicing. (NGUNI)

Nolwandle (f) One who lives near the seaside. (NGUNI)

Nolwazi (f) Mother of knowledge. (NGUNI)

Nomabhele (f) Daughter of 'Amabhele'. (NGUNI)

Nomaciko (f) One with attention to details. (NGUNI)

Nomafu (f) Of the clouds. *Born on a cloudy day.* (NGUNI)

Nomagcino (f) The last-born daughter. (NGUNI)

Nomagcisa (f) An expert woman. (NGUNI)

Nomagugu (f) Mother of treasures/precious things. (NGUNI)

Nomahawu (f) One who is shielded from danger. (NGUNI)

Nomahlubi (f) Daughter of the family of 'Amahlubi'. (NGUNI)

Nomahobe (f) Of the doves. (NGUNI)

Nomajama (f) Daughter of the family of 'Amajama'. (NGUNI)

Nomakhaya (f) Home woman. *Sometimes this name can be given to a new bride in her marital home.* (NGUNI)

Nomakholwa (f) Mother of believers. (NGUNI)

Nomakwezi (f) Star. (NGUNI)

Nomalanga (f) Of the day. (NGUNI)

Nomali (f) The lover of money. (NGUNI)

Nomalinge (f) Effort. *Name given after having made several efforts to conceive.* (NGUNI)

Nomalizo (f) Comforter. *A child may be born after a tragedy and will bring consolation.* (NGUNI)

Nomalungelo (f) Rights; one's own entitlement. (NGUNI)

Nomanini (f) Anytime. (NGUNI)

Nomaphelo (f) The last-born daughter. (NGUNI)

Nomaqabaka (f) One born during a cold spell. (NGUNI)

Nomaqiniso (f) One who sticks with the truth. (NGUNI)

Nomasabatha (f) Girl born on Saturday. (NGUNI)

Nomashingila (f) One who proudly walks away. (NGUNI)

Nomasirayeli (f) From the name 'Israel'. (NGUNI)

Nomasizwe (f) Mother of a nation. (NGUNI)

Nomasonto (f) Born on Sunday. (NGUNI)

Nomaswazi (f) Connected to the Swazi nation. (NGUNI)

Nomathalente (f) Mother of talents. (NGUNI)

Nomathamsanqa (f) Good fortune. (NGUNI)

Nomathanda (f) The one who loves. (NGUNI)

Nomathanxase (f) Without form, grace or poise. *This is a protective name, given to shield the child from evil intentions/spirits.* (NGUNI)

Nomathemba (f) One who is loyal and trustworthy. (NGUNI)

Nomatshawe (f) Princess daughter of the royal family 'Amatshawe'. (NGUNI)

Nomatshezi (f) Daughter of 'Amatshezi'. (NGUNI)

Nomatyala (f) The guilty one. *One who is constantly being accused of wrongdoing.* (NGUNI)

Nomawethu (f) One who belongs to us. (NGUNI)

Nomaweza (f) One who will cause us to cross over. (NGUNI)

Nomawezo (f) She will bring us across the rivers. (NGUNI)

Nomawuse (f) Daughter of 'Amawuse'. (NGUNI)

NomaWushe (f) Daughter of the Mawushe family. (NGUNI)

Nomaxabiso (f) Valued daughter. (NGUNI)

Nomaxhyifilili (f) Ugly and unappetizing. *Name given with the hope that it will protect the child against the evil eye.* (NGUNI)

Nomazizi (f) Daughter of 'Amazizi'. (NGUNI)

Nombeko (f) One who is well behaved. (NGUNI)

Nombizo (f) Girl born when there was a big royal meeting or 'imbizo'. (NGUNI)

Nombulelo (f) Thankful. (NGUNI)

Nombuso (f) Mother of the kingdom; joyous celebration. (NGUNI)

Nombuswana (f) Little mother of the kingdom. (NGUNI)

Nombuyiselo (f) Mother of restoration. (NGUNI)

Nombuzo (f) The questionable one. (NGUNI)

Nomcebo (f) With riches. (NGUNI)

Nomfanelo (f) Worthy of being loved. (NGUNI)

Nomfazwe (f) Mother of war. (NGUNI)

Nomfezeko (f) Accomplishment. (NGUNI)

Nomfundiso (f) See 'Nomfundo'.

Nomfundo (f) One who brings the lamp (light) of learning to the ignorant. (NGUNI)

Nomfuneko (f) She has been desired. (NGUNI)

Nomgcobo (f) The merry daughter. (NGUNI)

Nomgqibelo (f) Girl born on a Saturday ('Mgqibelo'). *This name can also be used to mean the last-born.* (NGUNI)

Nomhawu (f) One with compassion. (NGUNI)

Nomhlaba (f) Of the mother Earth. (NGUNI)

Nomhlanga (f) One who carries the reed in celebration of virginity. (NGUNI)

Nomhle (f) The pretty one. (NGUNI)

Nomhlekhabo (f) She who graces her home with beauty. (NGUNI)

Nomkhitha Nomi (f) The beautiful one; fair to look upon. (NGUNI)

Nomkhosi (f) The one who causes celebrations. (NGUNI)

Nomlomo (f) Big-mouthed one. *The mother used this name as an indirect communication to her sister in-law, who loved to gossip.* (NGUNI)

Nomnotho (f) Wealthy. (NGUNI)

Nomntu (f) Woman of humanity. (NGUNI)

Nomonde (f) Full of empathy and understanding. (NGUNI)

Nomoya (f) Born on a windy day. (NGUNI)

Nompazamo (f) One who has erred. *Name usually given for unplanned pregnancy.* (NGUNI)

Nompendulo (f) An answer. (NGUNI)

Nomphelo (f) The end. *Name given to the last child.* (NGUNI)

Nompiliso Nompi Nompilo (f) Healthy one. (NGUNI)

Nompumelelo (f) The successful one. (NGUNI)

Nomqhele (f) Mother of crowns. (NGUNI)

Nomqondiso (f) One who guides. (NGUNI)

Nomsa (f) One with grace or kindness. (NGUNI)

Nomthandazo (f) Mother of prayer. *The mother has prayed for either the birth of the child or the survival of the child.* (NGUNI)

Nomthetho (f) One with the law. (NGUNI)

Nomthunzi (f) Shade. (NGUNI)

Nomtsalane (f) Attractive and eye-catching beauty. (NGUNI)

Nomusa (f) Mother of grace and modesty. (NGUNI)

Nomvano (f) Agreeable. (NGUNI)

Nomveliso Nomvela (f) Appear. (NGUNI)

Nomvelo (f) Mother of nature. (NGUNI)

Nomvula (f) One born on a rainy day. (NGUNI)

Nomvulo (f) One born on a Monday. (NGUNI)

Nomvuselelo (f) One who revitalises and revives. (NGUNI)

Nomvuyiso Nomvuyo (f) One who causes rejoicing. (NGUNI)

Nomvuzo (f) Reward. (NGUNI)

Nomxolisi (f) Daughter who brings forgiveness. (NGUNI)

Nomzamo (f) The one who tries hard. (NGUNI)

Nomzi (f) One taking care of and strengthening the home. (NGUNI)

Nomzikazi (f) One taking care of a big home. (NGUNI)

Nonala (f) One who brings plentiful harvest. (NGUNI)

Nonceba (f) One full of mercy. (NGUNI)

Noncedo (f) Helpful one. (NGUNI)

Noncekelelo (f) The one who flatters. (NGUNI)

Noncwala (f) Of the Ncwala. *One born during 'Ncwala', which is a great Swazi first fruits feast.* (NGUNI)

Nondala (f) Of the Bushmen. (NGUNI)

Nondlela (f) The one who is nomadic. (NGUNI)

Nondumiso (f) Praise be to God. (NGUNI)

Nonduxu (f) Huge and ugly. *Protective name given to shield the child from the evil eye.* (NGUNI)

Nondyebo (f) Wealthy one. (NGUNI)

Nonetswa (f) Be anointed. *This is a blessing pronouncement.* (SOTHO)

Nongcebo (f) The one with riches. (NGUNI)

Nongenile (f) She has entered. (NGUNI)

Nongotela (f) Be very sweet. (NGUNI)

Nongotelile (f) Very sweet one. (NGUNI)

Nongqawuse (f) Away with falsehood. *This was the first name of a teenage prophetess of doom. Nongqawuse had a vision that the dead will arise if the Xhosa people were to kill their cattle, the Xhosa then began killing their own cattle in February 1856 but the dead did not rise.* (NGUNI)

Nonhlanhla Nonhla (f) Mother of good fortune. (NGUNI)

Nonhle (f) The beautiful one. (NGUNI)

Nonjabulo (f) Mother of joy. (NGUNI)

Nonkanyiso (f) One who brings light. (NGUNI)

Nonkazimlo (f) One with glory. (NGUNI)

Nonkenteza (f) One with a loud clamour. (NGUNI)

Nonkhulumo (f) She is their discussion. *The name-giver is expressing her awareness of what is going on behind her back.* (NGUNI)

Nonkosazana (f) *See 'Nkosazana'.*

Nonkosi (f) Of royalty. (NGUNI)

Nonkqubela (f) Have been longing for. (NGUNI)

Nonkululeko (f) Mother of freedom. (NGUNI)

Nonophile (f) Has increased in wealth. (NGUNI)

Nonoza (f) Sluggish one. (NGUNI)

Nonqaba (f) She is our place of safety. (NGUNI)

Nontandazo (f) *See 'Nomthandazo'.*

Nontando (f) One with love. (NGUNI)

Nontembeko (f)   One with hope and trust. (NGUNI)

Nontembiso (f)   One with a promise. (NGUNI)

Nontlanzeko (f)   The one who is very tidy and clean. (NGUNI)

Nontle (f)   Beautiful girl. (NGUNI)

Nontobeko (f)   The humbled and meek one. (NGUNI)

Nontokozo (f)   One filled with joyous gladness. (NGUNI)

Nontsapho (f)   With abundance. (NGUNI)

Nontsasa (f)   A girl born early in the morning. (NGUNI)

Nontshaba (f)   One with opponents. (NGUNI)

Nontshukumo (f)   The one who is active and lively. (NGUNI)

Nontsikelo (f)   Pillar. (NGUNI)

Nontsikizi (f)   Black bird. *Name given to a baby with a dark complexion.* (NGUNI)

Nontsizi (f)   Desolate woman. *Name-giver was experiencing much grief when this name was given.* (NGUNI)

Nontuthuko (f)   See 'Thuthuka'.

Nontuthuzelo (f)   One bringing us comfort. (NGUNI)

Nontutuzelo (f)   One who soothes the pain. (NGUNI)

Nontwingento (f)   Nothingness. *Name given with the hope that it will protect the child from the evil eye.* (NGUNI)

Nonyamezelo (f)   The persevering one. (NGUNI)

Nonyaniso (f)   One who is genuine. (NGUNI)

Nonyewe (f)   Mother of controversy. (NGUNI)

Nonzame (f)   The one who tries hard. (NGUNI)

Nonzukiso (f)   The one who is praiseworthy. (NGUNI)

Nonzwakazi (f)   Daughter of a special kind; fine looking. (NGUNI)

Nopasika (f)   Passover child; Easter child. (NGUNI)

Nophakela (f)   The one who dishes out for others. (NGUNI)

Nophumuzile (f)   Reliever. *Bridal name bestowed with the hope that the in-laws will now find time to rest from the home duties.* (NGUNI)

Nosicelo (f)   We had asked for her. (NGUNI)

Nosikumbuzo (f)   Reminder. (NGUNI)

Nosimanga (f)   One who brings astonishment. (NGUNI)

Nosimilo (f)   Woman with a steadfast character. (NGUNI)

Nosimo (f)   *See 'Simo'.*

Nosine (f)   Born on Thursday. (NGUNI)

Nosintu (f)   Woman with humanity. (NGUNI)

Nosiphiwo   Nosipo   Nosipho (f)   Mother of a gift. (NGUNI)

Nosisa (f)   The merciful one; kind one. (NGUNI)

Nosisekelo (f)   One who is a foundation to our home. (NGUNI)

Nosithembele (f)   *See 'Sithembele'.*

Nosiviwe (f)   We have been heard. (NGUNI)

Nosiyabonga (f)   We are thankful for her. (NGUNI)

Nosizo (f)   She is our help. (NGUNI)

Nosizwe (f)   A mother of the nation. (NGUNI)

Nothando (f)   With love. (NGUNI)

Nothani (f)   Be wealthy! (NGUNI)

Nothini   Nothi (f)   What does she say? (NGUNI)

Nothisile (f)   Has made us wealthy. *A child is considered to be a valuable addition to the home.* (NGUNI)

Nothuba (f)   Mother of chance. (NGUNI)

Notsasa (f)   Early morning baby. *Indicating the time of birth.* (NGUNI)

Notshaba (f)   Mother of enemies. (NGUNI)

Notsile (f)   Wealthy one. (NGUNI)

Novemba (f)   One born in November. (NGUNI)

Nowethu (f)   She is now one of us. (NGUNI)

Noxhanti (f)   A woman of influential position. *'Xhanti' is a forked post for a kraal gate.* (NGUNI)

Noxolo (f)   Peaceful. (NGUNI)

Nozala (f)   Male parent. (NGUNI)

Nozibele   Nozi (f)   Kind woman. (NGUNI)

Nozibulo (f)   The first born girl. (NGUNI)

Nozibusiso (f)   One with blessings. (NGUNI)

Nozicelo (f)   One who has repeatedly been requested. (NGUNI)

Nozindaba (f)   One who likes the news. (NGUNI)

Noziphiwo   Nozipho (f)   Mother of gifts. (NGUNI)

Nozizwe (f) The one who belongs to the nation. (NGUNI)

Nozolile (f) Mother of quietness. (NGUNI)

Nozukile (f) She has excelled. (NGUNI)

Nozuko (f) Gracious one. (NGUNI)

Nozwelakhe (f) Her land. (NGUNI)

Nqaba (m) Shelter. (NGUNI)

Nqabakazi (f) Strong tower. (NGUNI)

Nqabenhle (m) A strong tower; shelter. (NGUNI)

Nqabile Rare; valuable. (NGUNI)

Nqabisa Adding value. (NGUNI)

Nqoba Triumph over. *The name indicates the victory over challenges that were facing the name-giver.* (NGUNI)

Nqobangothando Conquered through love. (NGUNI)

Nqobani Conquer. (NGUNI)

Nqobile Nqobi She has conquered. (NGUNI)

Nqobizitha (m) One who will conquer our enemies. (NGUNI)

Nqubeko (m) Progress. (NGUNI)

Nsalo (f) Remainder. *The family might have experienced infant deaths. Such a name may be given to the surviving child.* (XITSONGA)

Nsaseko (f) Beauty. (XITSONGA)

Nsatimuni (f) What kind of wife? *Name used by the mother in-law as the expression of contempt and belittlement of the wife her son has chosen.* (XITSONGA)

Nshakazhogwe (m) Name of former Botswana chief. (SOTHO)

Nsikelelo The pillar of the home. (NGUNI)

Nsikiti The bug. *Name given with the hope that it will protect the child against the evil eye.* (XITSONGA)

Nsisi-munwe One hair only. (XITSONGA)

Nsitakalo Help. (NGUNI)

Nsizwa (m) All boys. (NGUNI)

Nsovo Grace. (XITSONGA)

Nsuku Days. (NGUNI)

Nsukukazifani Days are not the same. *To remind people that things do change.* (NGUNI)

Nsungukati (f) Old woman with authority. (XITSONGA)

Nswanzwi (m) Name of former Botswana chief. (SOTHO)

Ntaba (m) Mountain. (NGUNI)

Ntabakayikhonjwa (m) The mountain which cannot be pointed. *One who is feared greatly.* (NGUNI)

Ntabeni (m) In the mountains. (NGUNI)

Ntakuseni (m) Help me; lift me up. (TSHIVENDA)

Ntambudzeni (m) Abuse me. *The child bearing this name was born when somebody in the family was being ill-treated.* (TSHIVENDA)

Ntandazo (f) Prayer. *The parents believe that the child was obtained through prayer.* (NGUNI)

Ntando (f)   Self-will. (NGUNI)

Ntandoyenkosi (f)   It is the will of the Lord. (NGUNI)

Ntandoyesizwe (m)   This child is the will of the nation. (NGUNI)

Ntandoyethu (m)   Our will. (NGUNI)

Ntangadzeni   Accept me. (TSHIVENDA)

Ntantathile   One running to and fro with no clear purpose. (NGUNI)

Ntanyana   Little neck. *Traditional folktale name.* (NGUNI)

Ntatauwane   Monstrous being. *Protective name given after successive infant deaths.* (SOTHO)

Ntathu (f)   I have three girls. (NGUNI)

Ntatu (f)   The third one, or born on Wednesday. (NGUNI)

Ntebaleng (f)   Forget about me. (SOTHO)

Ntembeko (m)   Trust. (NGUNI)

Ntengo (m)   The highly prized one. (NGUNI)

Ntethelelo (m)   Forgiveness. (NGUNI)

Ntetjhana (m)   Small locust. *Name given to one with a small body frame.* (SOTHO)

Ntevheleni (m)   Follow me. (TSHIVENDA)

Ntfokoto (f)   Happiness. (NGUNI)

Nthabi (f)   Make me happy. (SOTHO)

Nthabiseng (f)   Make us happy. (SOTHO)

Nthaduleni (m)   Help me. (TSHIVENDA)

Nthambeleni (m) Hire people to kill me. *May refer to a situation where people are plotting to kill someone, and the name-giver will dare them to go ahead with their intention.* (TSHIVENDA)

Nthatisi   Nthati (f) One to love me. (SOTHO)

Nthetsheleseni (m) Listen to me. *Powerful and authoritative name originally used for chiefs.* (TSHIVENDA)

Nthlari (m) Bright; wise headed. (XITSONGA)

Nthofeela (m) Thing. *Such non-human names are usually replaced by meaningful names after initiation.* (SOTHO)

Nthupheni (m) Make me suffer. *Name-giver is venting their frustration over their situation.* (TSHIVENDA)

Nthuseni (m) Assist me; help me. (TSHIVENDA)

Ntiyiselo (m) Perseverance. (XITSONGA)

Ntiyiso (m) Truth. (XITSONGA)

Ntja (m) Dog. *Such non-human names are usually replaced by meaningful names after initiation.* (SOTHO)

Ntlafala (f) Become beautiful. (SOTHO)

Ntlalontle (f) Live well; social worker. (NGUNI)

Ntlanganiso (m) Bringing together. *Name given with the hope that the birth of a child will end conflicts within the family.* (NGUNI)

Ntlhamu (m) A trap. *Name given to warn the father that the mother used begetting a child to keep the man in the relationship.* (XITSONGA)

Ntlhari (m) Clever one. (XITSONGA)

Ntloko (m) Head; leader. (NGUNI)

Ntlumelo (m) A young shoot from an old stick. *Name can be given to a child who was given birth to by an older woman.* (NGUNI)

Ntobeko (m) Respect. (NGUNI)

Ntodeni (m) Find me; look for me. (TSHIVENDA)

Ntombazana (f) Little girl. (NGUNI)

Ntombekhaya **Ntombekaya** (f) Home girl. (NGUNI)

Ntombekwezi (f) Daughter of the morning. *Name can be given to a girl born at sunrise or the family may be meaning a new dawn in their lives.* (NGUNI)

Ntombenhle (f) Pretty girl. See 'Ntombentle'. (NGUNI)

Ntombenkosi (f) The girl belongs to the Lord. (NGUNI)

Ntombentle (f) Beautiful girl. (NGUNI)

Ntombentsha (f) It's a new girl. (NGUNI)

Ntombesibini (f) The second girl. (NGUNI)

Ntombesine (f) The fourth girl. (NGUNI)

Ntombesithathu (f) The third girl. (NGUNI)

Ntombesizwe (f) The girl belonging to our nation. (NGUNI)

Ntombethemba (f) The girl with hope. (NGUNI)

Ntombezinhle (f) Beautiful girls. (NGUNI)

Ntombi (f) Girl. *Usually refers to a mature girl.* (NGUNI)

Ntombifikile (f) The girl has arrived. (NGUNI)

Ntombifuthi (f) It's a girl again. *A combination of 'Ntombi' and 'Futhi'.* (NGUNI)

Ntombikababamkhulu (f) Grandfather's girl. (NGUNI)

Ntombikayise (f) Father's girl. *A combination of 'Ntombi' and 'Uyise'.* (NGUNI)

Ntombiko (f) The girl is here. (NGUNI)

Ntombithule (f) The quiet girl. (NGUNI)

Ntombiyakhe (f) Their girl. *A combination of 'Ntombi' and 'Yakhe'.* (NGUNI)

Ntombizakhe (f) His girls. (NGUNI)

Ntombizandile (f) The girls have increased. (NGUNI)

Ntombizanele (f) We have had enough girls. (NGUNI)

Ntombizethu (f) Our girl. (NGUNI)

Ntombizikhona (f) The girls are present. (NGUNI)

Ntombizine (f) There are now four girls. *Name reveals the quantity of births in the family.* (NGUNI)

Ntombizodidi (f) Precious girls. (NGUNI)

Ntombizodwa (f) Girls only. *Name reveals gender of children in the family.* (NGUNI)

Ntombizokhethelo (f) Special girl. (NGUNI)

Ntombokhanyo (f) Girl of the Light. (NGUNI)

Ntombomzi (f) She belongs to the home. (NGUNI)

Ntombovuyo (f) Girl who has brought rejoicing. (NGUNI)

Ntomboxolo (f) Girl who loves peace. *A combination of 'Ntombi' and 'Uxolo'.* (NGUNI)

Ntombozuko (f) Gracious woman. (NGUNI)

Ntondo The last-born child in a family. (NGUNI)

Ntoyonke Everything. *This child has been longed for and now that it is here, it is everything to the parents.* (NGUNI)

Ntozakhe His own things. (NGUNI)

Ntozimbi Things are out of shape. *The conditions, whether in the home or community, were unpleasant around the time of birth.* (NGUNI)

Ntozomntu His personal belongings. *From the expression 'Ungazithini Izinto zomntu', literally meaning: what can you do to someone else's things? It is a warning that you must take care of what is not yours.* (NGUNI)

Ntsakiso Delight. (XITSONGA)

Ntsako (f) Happiness. *The parents were happy to receive the birth of this girl.* (XITSONGA)

Ntsapho (f) Abundance. (NGUNI)

Ntsebo Name adapted from the word for 'whispers' (ntseba). *There must have been gossip going around at the time of birth.* (SOTHO)

Ntseiseni (m) Make me laugh. *This is a power name that dares those who are intending to do harm to the child.* (TSHIVENDA)

Ntshamela-Nkambana (m) Nickname for one who remains at home for the clay dish. *Name given to someone who stays home to do nothing but eat.* (XITSONGA)

Ntshamiseko (m) Stability. (XITSONGA)

Ntshavheni (m) Be afraid of me. *This name can be given to royalty and communicates the message that he must be revered.* (TSHIVENDA)

Ntshembexa (m) One not straight forward. (NGUNI)

Ntshembo (m) We have hope. (XITSONGA)

Ntshengedzeni Torture me. *This name is a form of communication when there is conflict in the community.* (TSHIVENDA)

Ntshuxeko Liberation. (XITSONGA)

Ntsieni Leave me. *A plea by the name-giver to be left alone or rather to be left in peace.* (TSHIVENDA)

Ntsika Pillar. *Name given with the hope that this child will bring stability in the home.* (NGUNI)

Ntsikayomzi Home pillar. (NGUNI)

Ntsikelelo Ntsike Blessings. (NGUNI)

Ntsikomzi *See 'Ntsikayomzi'.* (NGUNI)

Ntsokolo (m) Struggle. *There may be a situation or event in the home community or even in the nation where people are struggling to survive.* (NGUNI)

Ntsovelo (m) To reap. (XITSONGA)

Ntsu (m) Eagle. *The tendency to use animal names is due to the behaviour, personality and certain character traits which the name-bearer is thought to share with a specific animal.* (SOTHO)

Ntsumi (f) An angel. (XITSONGA)

Ntsundeni (f) Chase me away. *Daring those who were saying that she must be chased away since she cannot give birth.* (TSHIVENDA)

Ntswaki (f) Name given for the only girl among boys. (SOTHO)

Ntswebu Resemblance. (NGUNI)

Ntulizwe (m) The dust of the earth. *Such a name may be given to an illegitimate child.* (NGUNI)

Ntumbuloko Creation. (XITSONGA)

Ntungufhadzeni Make me sad; hurt me. *Name-giving is a chance to dare those who are ill-treating the name-giver.* (TSHIVENDA)

Ntuthuzelo Ntutuzelo Comfort. *Names such as this are given when the child is born after some misfortune.* (NGUNI)

Ntwanano Mutual understanding. (XITSONGA)

Ntyantyambo (f) Flower. (NGUNI)

Nunakulobye (m) Covenant. (XITSONGA)

Nwa (f) Child of. *Usually used as a prefix on their maiden name for married women.* (TSONGA) (VENDA)

Nwabisa (f) One who makes happy. (NGUNI)

Nwafunyunyu (f) Daughter of Funyunyu. *Bridal name that links her with her family (maiden) name.* (TSHIVENDA)

Nwagomodo (f) Daughter of the big forehead. (XITSONGA)

Nwakhadi (f) The daughter of Khadi. *Bridal name that associates her with her family (maiden) name.* (TSHIVENDA)

Nwakhakhu (f) The daughter of Khakhu. *Bridal name that associates her with her family (maiden) name* (TSHIVENDA)

Nwakhavana (f) Daughter of the little navel. (XITSONGA)

Nwakhwiri (f) Daughter of the belly. *Meaning the one I carried in my belly.* (XITSONGA)

Nwakuthlani (f) Premature baby girl. (XITSONGA)

Nwa-luva-tilo (f) The one who pays his tax to heaven. *Meaning he has received the favor because he has honored God.* (XITSONGA)

Nwamafela (f) Daughter born in death. *This name could be given after a difficult birth. Bearing in mind that often there will be no medical intervention, many women will lose their lives in giving birth.* (XITSONGA)

Nwamakatla (f) Daughter of the shoulders. (XITSONGA)

Nwamalengeti (f)   The daughter who caused tears. (XITSONGA)

Nwamanyelana (f)   Daughter of the one who went aside. *Given to an illegitimate child.* (XITSONGA)

Nwamaovakule (f)   Daughter of the one who pulled the branch far. *'Ku ova' means to pull the branch of a tree to oneself. The name is given to someone who has gone through trouble.* (XITSONGA)

Nwamarhumbana (f)   Daughter of the little bowels. (XITSONGA)

Nwamasaka (f)   Child of the bag. (XITSONGA)

Nwamatseve (f)   Daughter of the flanks. (XITSONGA)

Nwamavele (f)   Daughter of the breasts; the one who has sucked from the breast. (XITSONGA)

Nwamavoko (f)   Daughter of the arms; one who is held close. (XITSONGA)

Nwambenyana (f)   The one with the little handle. (XITSONGA)

Nwamisisi   Daughter of the hair. (XITSONGA)

Nwamixixi (f)   Daughter of the hair. *In the language of infants, Nwamisisi is pronounced 'xirimi' instead.* (XITSONGA)

Nwamuhambu (f)   The one of the sweet potato. *See 'Nwaxiketse'.* (XITSONGA)

Nwamutate (f)   The child of Mutate. (XITSONGA)

Nwanawatilo (f) Daughter of the heavens. (XITSONGA)

Nwandzandzana (f) Daughter of the 'ndzandzana' (creeping grass). (XITSONGA)

Nwandzumbi (f) Daughter of the thigh. *Meaning, my very own child.* (XITSONGA)

Nwanhlakwana (f) Daughter of the little head. (XITSONGA)

Nwanhonga (f) Daughter of the stick. (XITSONGA)

Nwanyana (f) Girl. (XITSONGA)

Nwaphamana (f) The one who is always caught. (XITSONGA)

Nwasundani (f) The daughter of Sundani. *Bridal name that links her with her family (maiden) name.* (TSHIVENDA)

Nwavembana (f) Daughter of the little cloth. (XITSONGA)

Nwaxihlokana (f) The little ax; the angry one. (XITSONGA)

Nwaxiketse (f) The one of the pineapple. *Apparently a sweet one! But it is not so, it is taken from a ritual of the Chopi people. When they commit murder, they dig a hole, bury the corpse and plant pineapples, the leaves of which are always green. So the meaning is the one who conceals things.* (XITSONGA)

Nwaxikundzu (f) Daughter of the stump. (XITSONGA)

Nwaxilatana (f) Daughter of the one who puts to sleep. (XITSONGA)

Nwaxintihwana (f) Daughter of the little finger. (XITSONGA)

Nwaxintsaka (f) Daughter of the one who spits or who despises. *The name may be given when a wife feels she is despised by her husband.* (XITSONGA)

Nwaxirhendze (f) Daughter of the heel. (XITSONGA)

Nwaxirhoxana (f) The little bitter lemon. (XITSONGA)

Nwaxisi (f) Daughter of the deceiver. (XITSONGA)

Nwaxivandla (f) Daughter of the place. (XITSONGA)

Nwedamhala (m) December. *Name can be given to a child born in December.* (XITSONGA)

Nweleziyahlehla (m) The hair is reversing. *Name given for someone with a bald head.* (NGUNI)

Nxaneliwe (m) Desired. *Parents have long desired a child.* (NGUNI)

Nxele (m) Left-handed one. (NGUNI)

Nxelezana (f) Left-handed girl. (NGUNI)

Nyabele (f) The mother of Bele. (TSHIVENDA)

Nyadenga (f) Mother of Denga. *Denga being the firstborn.* (TSHIVENDA)

Nyadombo (f) The mother of Dombo. *Dombo being the firstborn.* (TSHIVENDA)

Nyadzawela (m) Misfortune. *Taken from a proverb 'Nya Dzawela Vhanwe na sea matshelo zwi do ni welavho': Do not celebrate the misfortunes of others, for they may befall you as well.* (TSHIVENDA)

Nyakallo Joy. *Rejoicing at the birth of a child.* (SOTHO)

Nyakukolwe (m) The heron. (XITSONGA)

Nyakuvatle (m) The one that carves its head like a spoon i.e. the cobra. *Name derived from a praise poem.* (XITSONGA)

Nyaluvhani (f) Mother of Luvhani. *One who hero-worships another.* (TSHIVENDA)

Nyamasindi (f) The mother of Masindi. (TSHIVENDA)

Nyamayavo (m) Their meat. *Telling the messengers of death 'Here is your meat'. Usually this name is given after several infant deaths in the family.* (XITSONGA)

Nyameka (f) The one who endures. (NGUNI)

Nyameko Attentive and diligent one. (NGUNI)

Nyamologa Become happy/cheerful. (SOTHO)

Nyana (m) Son. (NGUNI)

Nyandi Good fortune. (TSHIVENDA)

Nyanga Moon; month; traditional healer. (NGUNI)

Nyaniso Of a truth. (NGUNI)

Nyapoga Revealed. (SOTHO)

Nyasivhavhone Do not be comforted. *From the proverb 'Nyasivhavhone Mano u seya mbilu dzavho dzi panda mahe': meaning, do not be comforted by the teeth that grin for you, for you do not know what is hidden away in the heart.* (TSHIVENDA)

Nyathela The daughter of the tax. *Born at the time of tax collecting.* (XITSONGA)

Nyatshinovhea The glue. *From the proverb 'Nyatshinovhela Tshi no vhea mudi ndi khana mapfufha a fhaladza mudi': meaning, The glue that holds a family together is the chest, talking with outsiders only breeds incoherence.* (TSHIVENDA)

Nyatshisevhe The mother of Tshisevhe. (TSHIVENDA)

Nyawaisedza One who gossips. *This personal name is derived from the idiomatic expression 'wa isedza munwe phungo na iwe i do u ela-vho': one who gossips, will be talked about also.* (TSHIVENDA)

Nyawasedza To defame. *Taken from the proverb 'Nyawasedza phungo mulanda na iwe mukoma i do u yela vho': meaning defaming one's subjects, defames oneself.* (TSHIVENDA)

Nyawelo Nyawe Rest. (TSHIVENDA)

Nyawukuwuku (m) The robin redbreast. *The tendency to use animal names is due to the behaviour, personality and certain character traits which the name-bearer is thought to share with a specific animal.* (XITSONGA)

Nyeleti A shining star. (XITSONGA)

Nyemulo Desire. (XITSONGA)

Nyenyedzi Star. (TSHIVENDA)

Nyikadzino (m) Our land. (TSHIVENDA)

Nyikiwe (f) Gifted. (XITSONGA)

Nyiko Gift. (XITSONGA)

Nyimbana (f) Little womb. (XITSONGA)

Nyobisa (f) Make joyful. (NGUNI)

Nyokahansi Snake in the grass. *Name given to a shrewd person.* (XITSONGA)

Nyokanyana The little snake. *The tendency to use animal names is due to the behaviour, personality and certain character traits which the name-bearer is thought to share with a specific animal. A snake is known for being a clever and deceitful creature.* (XITSONGA)

Nyokasana *See 'Nyokasi'.* (XITSONGA)

Nyokasi The little snake. *The tendency to use animal names is due to the behaviour, personality and certain character traits which the name-bearer is thought to share with a specific animal; a snake is known for being a clever and deceitful creature.* (XITSONGA)

Nzeku (m) A distinguished man. (NGUNI)

Nzondelelo (m) *See 'Nzondo'.*

Nzondo (m) Hatred. (NGUNI)

Nzuzenhle (m) A good gain. (NGUNI)

Nzuzo (m) Gain. *The birth of the child signifies gain in the family.* (NGUNI)

Nzwakazi Nzwa (f) The beauty or princess of the home. (NGUNI)

Oagile (m) The household has been firmly built. (SOTHO)

Oaitse (m) God knows. (SOTHO)

Oarona (m) Ours. (SOTHO)

Oatile (m) Has built. *Alternative form of 'Oagile'.* (SOTHO)

Obakeng (m) Praise God. (SOTHO)

Obonye (m) He has seen. (SOTHO)

Odirile (m) He has done/created/made. (SOTHO)

Oduetse (m) He has paid. (SOTHO)

Odwa (m) Only. (NGUNI)

Ofentse (m) Victory won. (SOTHO)

Ogomoditse (m) He has comforted. *Born after the mother had several miscarriages.* (SOTHO)

Ohentshe (m) Has won a victory. (SOTHO)

Okuhle (m) That which is good. (NGUNI)

Okwakhe (m) Belonging to him or her. (NGUNI)

Okwethu (m) Our belonging (possession). (NGUNI)

Olebile (m) He (God) is watching. (SOTHO)

Olebogeng (m) Thank Him (God). (SOTHO)

Olwethu Olwetu Ours. (NGUNI)

Omelezekiswa Be encouraged. (NGUNI)

Omelezilisa Be encouraged. (NGUNI)

Omhle (f) Beautiful. (NGUNI)

Omphile (f) I have been freely given. (SOTHO)

Onalenna He (God) is with me. (SOTHO)

Ondela Look steadily at. (NGUNI)

Onesimo Well-behaved one. (NGUNI)

Onesipho One with a gift. (NGUNI)

Onesisa One with mercy. (NGUNI)

Ongama Taking charge of; rule over. (NGUNI)

Onke All. (NGUNI)

Onkemetse (m) He (God) is representing me. (SOTHO)

Onkgopotse (m) He (God) remembered me. (SOTHO)

Onolufefe (f) One with grace. (NGUNI)

Onothando (f) One with love. (NGUNI)

Onoxolo (f) One with forgiveness. (NGUNI)

Ontibile (f) He (God) is watching over me. (SOTHO)

Ontiretse He (God) has done it for me. (SOTHO)

Ontlametse He (God) has protected and taken care of me. (SOTHO)

Opedisa I have a reason to sing. (SOTHO)

Orifha He (God) gave us this child. (TSHIVENDA)

Osisipho This one is a gift. *Derived from the belief that a child is a gift from God.* (NGUNI)

Oteng He (God) is there. (SOTHO)

Othembela Trust in. (NGUNI)

Othembele One who is trusting. (NGUNI)

Othusitse (m) He has helped. (SOTHO)

Otsile (m) He has come. (SOTHO)

Oupanyana (m) Small grandfather. (SOTHO)

Owethu *Same as 'Olwethu'.* (NGUNI)

Oyamile One that is depending on us. (NGUNI)

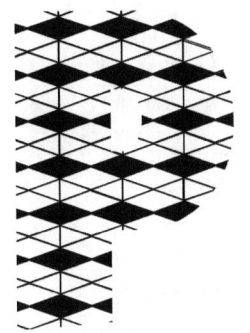

Paballo (m) Protection. (SOTHO)

Pahla (m) First born identical boy twin. (XITSONGA)

Pahlazi (f) First born identical girl twin. (XITSONGA)

Paki (m) Witness. (NGUNI)

Pako (m) Glory to God. (SOTHO)

Palesa (f) Flower. (SOTHO)

Paolosi (m) Small; little. *Sotho name of biblical origin, derived from Paul.* (SOTHO)

Papama (f) *See 'Phaphama'.*

Pateka (f) Be cared for. (NGUNI)

Pathiswa Patiswa (f) One who carries the responsibility. (NGUNI)

Patuxolo The carrier of reconciliation. (NGUNI)

Peano Agreement. (SOTHO)

Pekentsha Cause to shine/reflect. (SOTHO)

Pekenya Cause to shine. (SOTHO)

Pelohlomogi Kind; merciful. (SOTHO)

Pelokgale Bold one. (SOTHO)

Pelonolo Kind. (SOTHO)

Pendela Concluded. *This name is given to the last child.* (TSHIVENDA)

Pendulwa Have been answered. *The family was praying for the child.* (NGUNI)

Peterose (m) A rock or stone. *Sotho name of biblical origin, derived from Peter.* (SOTHO)

Pfano (m) Agreement. (TSHIVENDA)

Pfarelo Pfare (m) Forgiveness. (TSHIVENDA)

Pfariso (m) Help. (TSHIVENDA)

Pfeledza (m) Satisfied. (TSHIVENDA)

Pfelela (m) Be satisfied. (TSHIVENDA)

Pfesesa (m) Appreciate. (TSHIVENDA)

Pfongologohlo (m) The crash of the door broken open. *This name can be given for news of an unexpected pregnancy.* (XITSONGA)

Pfuka (m) Arise. (XITSONGA)

Pfukile (m) Excited. (XITSONGA)

Pfuluwani (m) Relocate. *This name was bestowed on a child who was born when people were forcibly removed from their land by the apartheid government in 1966 and forced to settle elsewhere.* (TSHIVENDA)

Pfuma Become rich. (TSHIVENDA)

Pfumelela Allow; permit. (XITSONGA)

Pfumisa Enrich. (TSHIVENDA)

Pfunzo A lesson. (TSHIVENDA)

Phadima Shine; glitter. (SOTHO)

Phaello Profit. (SOTHO)

Phagameng Phagame Be raised/lifted. *The birth of a child gives a mother an elevated status within the home and community at large.* (SOTHO)

Phagamego Phagamilego Phagamile (f) Elevated. *See Phagameng.* (SOTHO)

Phahamo Eminence. *See Phagameng.* (SOTHO)

Phakama Phaka Be lifted up. *See Phagameng.* (NGUNI)

Phakamile (m) The exalted one. (NGUNI)

Phakamisa Phakanyiswa One who has been lifted up. *Same meaning as above* (NGUNI)

Phangami (m) Leader. (TSHIVENDA)

Phangela (m) Run in front of. (NGUNI)

Phangweni (m) In the act of carrying away. *The child was born when the family was moving.* (XITSONGA)

Phaphama Awake; arise. (NGUNI)

Phasika (m) Passover. *Name for the Passover child.* (NGUNI)

Phatheka The one who is being carried. (NGUNI)

Phathi Phathile Have handled. (NGUNI)

Phathiswa (m) One who is holding someone for someone else. (NGUNI)

Phathizizwe (m) Holding the nations. (NGUNI)

Phathutshedzo Phathu (m) Blessings. (TSHIVENDA)

Phedzi (m) Finish. *Given to the last-born child.* (TSHIVENDA)

Phejana The youngest child in the family. (SOTHO)

Pheko Remedy; cure. (SOTHO)

Phelela Phelelisa (f) To complete. *Name usually given to the last-born.* (NGUNI)

Pheliswa Phelisa (f) To make an end. *See Phelela.* (NGUNI)

Phelokazi (f) The last girl born. (NGUNI)

Phembeledzo (m) Appeasement. (TSHIVENDA)

Phendula (m) Answer. (NGUNI)

Phenyo (m) One who is victorious. (SOTHO)

Phephelaphi Where do we seek refuge? *When the birth of a child coincides with a calamity that has befallen a family.* (NGUNI)

Phephile (f) Safe and sheltered. (NGUNI)

Phephisani (f) Be consoled. (NGUNI)

Phethile (f) Have completed. *Usually given to the last-born child.* (NGUNI)

Phethisi (f) Completion; execution. *Usually given to the last-born child.* (SOTHO)

Phetho (m) The end. *Usually given to the last-born child.* (NGUNI)

Phetoho Phetogo (m) Change. (SOTHO)

Phetsile (f) The one who concludes. *The last-born child usually bears this name.* (NGUNI)

Phetuxolo Peace carrier. (NGUNI)

Phezisa (m) Complete. *The completeness of family.* (NGUNI)

Phikani (m) Deny him. *This name is meant to dare the father to deny a child who resembles him completely.* (NGUNI) (TSONGA)

Phila (m) Live. *The name is a blessing on the new life.* (NGUNI)

Philangani How will she live? *Poverty-stricken homes look at the child, wondering how they will support the child. Usually this name is given by grandmothers who are already supporting too many grandchildren by themselves.* (NGUNI)

Philangenkosi He is alive because of God. *The father was seriously ill when this child was born but recovered well. This name is to commemorate the father's healing.* (NGUNI)

Philani You must live. (NGUNI)

Philasande Live and increase. (NGUNI)

Philile Phili (f) She is alive. (NGUNI)

Philisa (f) Cause life. (NGUNI)

Philisiwe (f) Has been made alive. (NGUNI)

Philiswa (f) One who has been healed and made well. (NGUNI)

Phindile Phindi (f) Once again; repetition. (NGUNI)

Phindiwe (f) Replication. (NGUNI)

Phindulo Answer. (TSHIVENDA)

Phiwamandla Phiwa We have been empowered. (NGUNI)

Phiwokazi Phiwo (f) Great gift. (NGUNI)

Phiwokuhle (f) We have a goodly heritage. (NGUNI)

Phiwokwakhe (f) He who was given what was rightfully his. *At the time of birth the father received his portion of inheritance.* (NGUNI)

Phiwumusa Phiwe (f) We have been given grace. (NGUNI)

Phokgo Champion. (SOTHO)

Phoko Rumor. (SOTHO)

Pholile Pholi Soft and kind-hearted. (NGUNI)

Phologile Phologa Was rescued. (SOTHO)

Pholosa Salvation. (SOTHO)

Pholositse Cause to escape. (SOTHO)

Pholoso Saving; salvation. (SOTHO)

Phomola Rest. (SOTHO)

Phomolo Rest; relaxation. (SOTHO)

Phongiphayo I give to those who give to me. (NGUNI)

Phonoyi Elegant one. (NGUNI)

Phoshozwayo (f) Traditional folktale name. *Given as a nickname to someone who is talkative.* (NGUNI)

Phozisa (f) The one who soothes the pain. (NGUNI)

Phularo (f) A return; a comeback. *When a child resembles a dead relative.* (SOTHO)

Phumaho (f) Rich. (TSHIVENDA)

Phumaphi (f) Where from? *An unexpected pregnancy will raise this question.* (NGUNI)

Phumega (f) Be delicate. (SOTHO)

Phumelela Be successful. (NGUNI)

Phumelele Have succeeded. (NGUNI)

Phumelelo Achievement. (NGUNI)

Phumelo An outcome. (NGUNI)

Phumeza (f) The one who has brought us out of trouble. (NGUNI)

Phumla (f) Rest. (NGUNI)

Phumlile (f) Has rested. (NGUNI)

Phumlisa (f) Relieve someone. (NGUNI)

Phumlo Repose. (NGUNI)

Phumudzo Consolation and comfort. (TSHIVENDA)

Phumula (f) See 'Pumla'.

Phumza (f) Relieve. (NGUNI)

Phumzile Phumu Cause to rest. *A mother was burning with a desire to have this child, when it happened, it was a huge relief.* (NGUNI)

Phungo Rumour. (TSHIVENDA)

Phusu Disturbance. *Name given to protect the child against an evil eye.* (TSHIVENDA)

Phusuphusu Problems. *Circumstances surrounding the birth were troublesome.* (TSHIVENDA)

Phutheho Congregation; collection. (SOTHO)

Pikana Bantam chicken. *Name given to one with a small body frame.* (SOTHO)

Pikinini (f)   The little one. (NGUNI)

Pilasande (m)   Live and increase. (NGUNI)

Pima (m)   Measure. (XITSONGA)

Pimani (m)   Measure. (XITSONGA)

Pinda   Again. (NGUNI)

Pindile (f)   Has done it again. (NGUNI)

Pindiwe (f)   *See 'Phindiwe'.*

Pitso (m)   The chosen one; called one. (SOTHO)

Poelo (m)   Return; profit. (SOTHO)

Polelo (m)   Report. (SOTHO)

Poloko (m)   To be in safety. (SOTHO)

Polomashwashe   Polo (m)   Alligator. (SOTHO)

Pono (m)   Sight. (SOTHO)

Pont'so   Pontsho (m)   Vision; revelation. (SOTHO)

Popi (f)   A doll. (NGUNI)

Posita (f)   From the English 'Post'. *A story is relayed regarding a man who named his daughter Posita. His wife had had an affair with another man whilst he was away working in the Johannesburg mines. When he found the child on his return, he decided to call her 'Posita' meaning he made his wife pregnant through the post.* (XITSONGA)

Potego   Reliability. (SOTHO)

Pozisa   Someone who will bring soothing. *A child born after the family has experienced some tragedy.* (NGUNI)

Pshatlega   Fragile; breakable. (SOTHO)

Pula Rain. *See also 'Pulane', 'Pule', 'Puleng'.* (SOTHO)

Pulane Rainy. (SOTHO)

Pule Rainy; in the rain. (SOTHO)

Puleng (f) Born in or during the rain. (SOTHO)

Pumela (f) To come out. (NGUNI)

Pumeza (f) *See 'Phumeza'.*

Pumla (f) Rest. (NGUNI)

Pumlile (f) Have rested. (NGUNI)

Pumza (f) *See 'Phumeza'.*

Pumzile *See 'Phumeza'.* (NGUNI)

Puseletso Repeat. (SOTHO)

Puthuma Hurry up. (NGUNI)

Qaliwe He is looked at. (NGUNI)

Qanda Egg. *When the mother was weak and fragile during the pregnancy.* (NGUNI)

Qaphela Watch out! (NGUNI)

Qhakazile Qhaka (f) The flower has blossomed. (NGUNI)

Qhamani (m) Produce plentifully. (NGUNI)

Qhamisa Make fruitful. (NGUNI)

Qhamukephi Qhamu Where do you come from? *Name given by the grandfather after his daughter went to school away from home and came back heavily pregnant.* (NGUNI)

Qhamukile (f) She has appeared. (NGUNI)

Qhawe (m) The champion. (NGUNI)

Qhawekazi (f) The champion of champions. (NGUNI)

Qhelisiwe (f) Have been crowned. (NGUNI)

Qhololethu (f) Our pride. (NGUNI)

Qhubani Qhuba (m) Cause improvement. (NGUNI)

Qhubekani (m) Advancement. (NGUNI)

Qhubekile (f) Have advanced. (NGUNI)

Qina (m) Be strong. (NGUNI)

Qinisela Qiniselani Perseverance and persistence. (NGUNI)

Qiniso Qini The true one; true to self and to others. (NGUNI)

Qondakele Understandable. *This name may be a part of an ongoing dialogue about the situation surrounding the birth.* (NGUNI)

Qondani Be with understanding. (NGUNI)

Qondeni What is your intention? *In this case, the father threatened to chase the mother away. By using this name for her child she is responding to that threat.* (NGUNI)

Qondile Straight forward. (NGUNI)

Qophelo The highest standards. (NGUNI)

Qubeka (m) Progress. (NGUNI)

Qubekani (m) Go ahead. (NGUNI)

Qubeza (m) Diligent. (NGUNI)

Qukeza (m) Be diligent. (NGUNI)

Qwebeda (m) A determined person. (NGUNI)

Rabela Rabe (m) Pray. (TSHIVENDA)

Rabelani (m) Pray. (TSHIVENDA)

Rabvuma (m) Name of former chief of the Vendas. (TSHIVENDA)

Ralebitso (m) Father of Lebitso. (SOTHO)

Raluswielo (m) The one who is a broom; will sweep out evil. *Name from a praise poem.* (TSHIVENDA)

Ramabulana (m) One who plans well; can also mean the treacherous one. (TSHIVENDA)

Ramaneella (m) Moshoeshoe's (former Sotho chief) nephew. (SOTHO)

Ramano (m) Planner. (SOTHO)

Ramasia (m) Commemorating the grandfather. (SOTHO)

Ramathe (m) Father of Mathe. (SOTHO)

Ramatjato (m) Father of agility. *From 'tjato': meaning agility.* (SOTHO)

Ramatla (m) The one with strength. *Originally from the word 'matla': which means strength.* (SOTHO)

Ramawa (m) Diviner. (TSHIVENDA)

Rambado (m) One who prefers to fight with an axe or one who owns an axe. (TSHIVENDA)

Ramohato (m) Father of Mohato. (SOTHO)

Ramohau (m) Father of Mohau. (SOTHO)

Ramona (m) Self-seeking. (SOTHO)

Ramosa (m) The merciful one. (SOTHO)

Ranwedzi (m) New moon. *Taken from the proverb 'Ranwedzi muswa mutshenela vhakule vha haya vha tshi sala maswiswini': meaning the new moon glows for those far off whilst darkness greets us here.* (TSHIVENDA)

Rapitso (m) Father of Pitso. (SOTHO)

Rasila (m) One who likes to be smartly dressed or one who owns smart clothing. (TSHIVENDA)

Rata To want. (SOTHO)

Ratang Who loves. (SOTHO)

Rate Must love/like. (SOTHO)

Ratetsa Maintain; support. (SOTHO)

Rato Love. (SOTHO)

Ratsale (m) Father-in-law. (SOTHO)

Ratsebe (m) Name given for one with large ears. (SOTHO)

Ratsebo (m) The knowledgeable one. *Originally from the word 'tsebo' which means knowledge.* (SOTHO)

Ratshinyiwaho (m) Do whatever you want to do. *This name is given to a headman. It refers to a situation that prevailed when the headman was installed.* (TSHIVENDA)

Ratu (f) My love. (SOTHO)

Ratwa (f) One who is much loved. (SOTHO)

Raulinga (m) One who likes to test other people. (TSHIVENDA)

Reabetsoe Reabetswe (m) We have been provided for. (SOTHO)

Reabiloe Reabilwe (f) We have been blessed. (SOTHO)

Reaboka (f) We are full of praise. (SOTHO)

Realeboha (f) We are thankful. (SOTHO)

Refilwe Refiloe (f) We have been given. (SOTHO)

Relebohile Relebogile (f) We are grateful. (SOTHO)

Remaketse (f) Came to us by surprise. (SOTHO)

Rendani Rendi (f) Give praises. (TSHIVENDA)

Reneilwe (f) We have been given. *This name is in accord with the belief that children are a gift from God.* (SOTHO)

Reta (f) Praise; recite. (SOTHO)

Rethabile (f) We are happy. (SOTHO)

Rhandzani (f) One with love. (XITSONGA)

Rhandzavanhu (f) One who loves people. (XITSONGA)

Rhandzeka (f) Lovely. (XITSONGA)

Rhandzu (f) Love. (XITSONGA)

Rholihlahla (m) Pulling a branch of a tree. *Given to someone who has gone through a lot of trouble, or a troublemaker.* (NGUNI)

Rhulani (m) Bringer of peace. (XITSONGA)

Rido (m) Short form of 'Ridovhona'. (TSHIVENDA)

Ridomushumela (m) We will work for Him. *The parents are using this name as a reminder of their commitment to work for God.* (TSHIVENDA)

Ridovhona (m) We will see. *This name-giver is issuing a warning.* (TSHIVENDA)

Rifumuni (m) What type of death? *This is a protective name, after successive infant deaths.* (XITSONGA)

Rihiseriwa (m) Be avenged. (XITSONGA)

Rikotso Youngest child in the family. (XITSONGA)

Rinae (m) We are with Him. (TSHIVENDA)

Ringanisa (m) Make equal. (XITSONGA)

Risana (m) Baby boy. (XITSONGA)

Risenga (f) The bracelet. (XITSONGA)

Ritlatla (f) The heavy copper ring. *In the olden days, heavy copper rings were used as a means of exchange or for 'lobola'.* (XITSONGA)

Rivangavanga The tall one. (XITSONGA)

Rivata Cause to forget. (XITSONGA)

Rivhaningo Light. (XITSONGA)

Rofhiwa (f) We have been given. (TSHIVENDA)

Rolihlahla (m) See 'Rholihlahla'.

Ronewa We are given. (TSHIVENDA)

Rorisang **Rorisa** Praise. (SOTHO)

Rotshidziwa We are sanctified. *Through this personal name the name-giver conveys that they are dedicating their child to God.* (TSHIVENDA)

Rudzani (m) Cheer up. *To console someone who had bad experiences.* (TSHIVENDA)

Ruthe (f) Drunk; satisfied. *Sotho name of biblical origin, derived from Ruth.* (SOTHO)

Rwesa Help to carry a burden or a load. (SOTHO)

S'thembiso (m) Promise. (NGUNI)

Sabatha (m) Born on Saturday. (NGUNI)

Sabela Respond to the call. *Parenthood is regarded as a call.* (NGUNI)

Sabelesihle Good heritage. (NGUNI)

Sabelile The one who has responded when called. (NGUNI)

Sabelo (m) An inheritance. (NGUNI)

Sabelosami (m) My heritage. (NGUNI)

Sabelosamisihle (m) My substantial heritage. (NGUNI)

Sabo (m) Theirs. (NGUNI)

Sakaria (m) Memory of the Lord. *Sotho name of biblical origin, derived from Zachariah.* (SOTHO)

Sakhamuti (m) Head of a household; citizen. (NGUNI)

Sakhamzi (m) Citizen. (NGUNI)

Sakhekile (m) We have been built up. (NGUNI)

Sakhele (m) Built for us. (NGUNI)

Sakhelene (m) We are building near each other. (NGUNI)

Sakhile (m) We have built. (NGUNI)

Sakhiwo (m) Shelter or building. (NGUNI)

Sakhumzi Sakumzi Saki (m) We are building a home not just a house. *A combination of 'Sakha' and 'Umuzi'.* (NGUNI)

Salakutyelwa Salakutjelwa (m) Obstinate person. *Name from a proverb 'Isalakutjelwa sibona ngomopho': Meaning, He who refuses to take advise will suffer unpleasant consequences.* (NGUNI)

Salamahlangeni (m) One who remains in the reeds, that is after harvest. *Name given to a spinster.* (XITSONGA)

Salelo The remnant. (NGUNI)

Sambulo The revelation of what has been concealed. (NGUNI)

Sametsa (m) Support. (SOTHO)

Samuele (m) Heard of God; asked of God. *Sotho name of biblical origin, derived from Samuel.* (SOTHO)

Samukele Samke We have received. (NGUNI)

Samukelisiwe Samu (f) We have been allowed to receive. (NGUNI)

Samukeliso Samkelo See 'Samukelisiwe'. (NGUNI)

Sandhlana (m) The little palm of the hand. (XITSONGA)

Sandile Sandi (m) We have increased. (NGUNI)

Sandzisiwe Sandisiwe (f) We have been increased. (NGUNI)

Sandziso Sandiso (m) Increase. (NGUNI)

Sandiswa (f) Increased. (NGUNI)

Sandlasenkosi (m) The hand of God. (NGUNI)

Sandulele (m) Go before us; lead us. (NGUNI)

Sanele (f) We have enough. (NGUNI)

Sanelisiwe (f) We are satisfied. (NGUNI)

Saneliso Cause for satisfaction. (NGUNI)

Sankatana Senkatana (m) Boy. *Hero in many Basotho legendary folktales.* (SOTHO)

Sati (m) Knowledgeable person. (NGUNI)

Sazi (m) Get acquainted with us. (NGUNI)

Sbali (m) My brother-in-law. (NGUNI)

Sbongile (f) We have thanked. (NGUNI)

Sbongiseni (m) Let us all be grateful. (NGUNI)

Sbukiso Our show. (NGUNI)

Sbuko Mirror. *Child may resemble someone in the family.* (NGUNI)

Sbusile We are reigning. (NGUNI)

Sbusiso Sbu (m) A blessing. (NGUNI)

Sdudla A plump person. (NGUNI)

Sdudula (f) One with curves, beauty with a traditional African figure. (NGUNI)

Seani (m) Laugh. (TSHIVENDA)

Seapei (f) A cooker. (SOTHO)

Sea-sea Keep on laughing. (TSHIVENDA)

Sebare (m) Brother-in-law. (SOTHO)

Sebenzile Work well done. (NGUNI)

Seboga Have a vision. (SOTHO)

Sebogegi (f) An attractive one. (SOTHO)

Sebolai (m) Killer. (SOTHO)

Seboloki (m) Keeper; protector. (SOTHO)

Sebotse (f) Beautiful. (SOTHO)

Sebueng (m) Hold your peace. (SOTHO)

Sechaba Setjhaba (m) Nation. (SOTHO)

Sedifatsa Become illuminated. (SOTHO)

Seeiso (m) Name of the former principal chief of the Basotho. (SOTHO)

Seeng (m) Gone; gone astray. (SOTHO)

Sefako (m) Hailstone. *It was raining with hailstones during his birth.* (SOTHO)

Segametsi Sega (m) The vessel or calabash for drawing water. (SOTHO)

Segela (m) Support. (SOTHO)

Segofala (m) Be blessed; become happy. (SOTHO)

Segomotso (m) The object with which I am being comforted. (SOTHO)

Segosi (m) Royal; kingly; majestic. (SOTHO)

Sei (m) Amused. (TSHIVENDA)

Seka (m) Try a case; judge. (SOTHO)

Sekeliwe (f) The one who is supported. (NGUNI)

Sekgolokgotjhane (m) Wanderer. (SOTHO)

Sekgosi (m) Royal; kingly. (SOTHO)

Sello (m) There is mourning; a cry. *Probably born soon after a death in the family.* (SOTHO)

Seloba (m) Tribute; bribe; gift; levy. (SOTHO)

Sematlho (m) It (the baby) has eyes. (SOTHO)

Senamile (f) We are happy. (NGUNI)

Senamolelwa Redeemed. (SOTHO)

Senate (f) Mother of King Moshoeshoe II. (SOTHO)

Senele We are sufficient. *Declaring that the family is satisfied with the number of children they have.* (NGUNI)

Sengenedza Tickle. (TSHIVENDA)

Sengetile We have added on. (NGUNI)

Sengiphile (m) I have already given. (NGUNI)

Sengiphiwe (m) We have been given. (NGUNI)

Senzakahle Senzangakhona (m) We are doing well. (NGUNI)

Senzekile (m) It happened. (NGUNI)

Senzeni (m) What have we done? *The name-giver is addressing those who are mistreating them.* (NGUNI)

Senzile (m) We have done it. (NGUNI)

Senzo (m) A deed. (NGUNI)

Senzwesihle (m) A good deed. (NGUNI)

Seruô (m) Riches. (SOTHO)

Sesate (m) Royal; protocol. (SOTHO)

Sesi (f) Sister. (NGUNI)

Sethunya (f) A flower. *Making an appearance/allusion.* (SOTHO)

Setlhana (f) Yellow baby girl. *This name refers to the colour of the child's skin.* (SOTHO)

Setlogolo (m) Nephew. (SOTHO)

Setshegetso A support. (SOTHO)

Sewela (f) The only girl in a family of boys. (NGUNI)

Sewelabatho (f) Faith. (SOTHO)

Shadile (f) Has been wedded. *The mother got married while pregnant and the name was given to commemorate that event.* (NGUNI)

Shaka (m) Intestinal parasite; bastard; illegitimate child. *First name of Zulu king (1787–1828) who was known for being a bold warrior.* (NGUNI)

Shalazile (f) Have blushed. (NGUNI)

Shandu Shandukani (m) Change. (TSHIVENDA)

Shavha (m) Run away. (TSHIVENDA)

Shavhi Shavhelafhi (m) Where do we run to? (TSHIVENDA)

Shikombiso (m) Example. (XITSONGA)

Shiluva (f) A flower. (XITSONGA)

Shimisana Help each other in work. (TSHIVENDA)

Shivilelo Worry. (XITSONGA)

Shiyiwe (f) One who has been left behind. (NGUNI)

Shlobosenkosi (m) King's relative. (NGUNI)

Shoeshoe (m) Flower from the 'tsikitlane' plant: *Hypoxis argentea*. (SOTHO)

Shoni Shame. *Protective name.* (TSHIVENDA)

Shonisani Embarrass them. *Name employed as a communicative strategy by the name-giver.* (TSHIVENDA)

Shudufhadza Make happy. (TSHIVENDA)

Shuma Shumani Work. *At the birth of the child, the parents made a vow to work for the Lord.* (TSHIVENDA)

Sia Run away. *This may be given as advice to the mother to run away from her in-laws when the paternity of the child is questionable.* (SOTHO)

Siame Born under fine conditions. (SOTHO)

Sibabalwe (f) We have received favor. (NGUNI)

Sibahle (f) We are beautiful. (NGUNI)

Sibakhombisile (f) We have shown them. (NGUNI)

Sibani Lamp. (NGUNI)

Sibanisami (m) My lamp. (NGUNI)

Sibanisenkosi (m) Light-bringer for the Lord. (NGUNI)

Sibhombo (m) Big and heavy boy. (NGUNI)

Sibongile Sibo Sibongi (f) We give thanks. (NGUNI)

Sibongiseni (m) Join us in giving thanks. (NGUNI)

Sibonise (m) Show us the way. *Reflect the future responsibility of the child* (NGUNI)

Sibonisiwe (f) We have been advised. (NGUNI)

Siboniso (m) Advice. (NGUNI)

Sibulele (m) We are thankful. (NGUNI)

Sibusile (f) We have reigned. (NGUNI)

Sibusisiwe (f) We have been blessed. (NGUNI)

Sibusiso (m)   Blessing; blessed. (NGUNI)

Sicakazana (f)   A servant girl. (NGUNI)

Sicakucaku   One who is very showy. (NGUNI)

Sicebi   The rich one. (NGUNI)

Sicebile   We have been enriched. (NGUNI)

Sicelankobe   One asking for 'izinkobe' (dried corn). *It used to be eaten as a snack. This is often a name given to a poor person.* (NGUNI)

Sicelizapholo (m)   One who asks for milk at milking time. *This name was given to a poor person who had no cows of their own to milk.* (NGUNI)

Sicelo   A request. *The parents had prayed for the child.* (NGUNI)

Sidinile   We have been burdened. (NGUNI)

Sidzingo   Necessity. (NGUNI)

Sifikile   We have arrived. (NGUNI)

Sifiso (m)   A wish. *Name given to the child when the family had wished for a boy and the wish was granted.* (NGUNI)

Sifubasibanzi (m)   Broad-chested one. (NGUNI)

Sifundo (m)   A lesson learnt. *Usually associated with teenage pregnancy.* (NGUNI)

Sigantsula (m)   A bold and insolent one. (NGUNI)

Sigcinile   We have ended. (NGUNI)

Sigidi (m)   A very large number. (NGUNI)

Sigonyela (m) Brave and daring one. *Name of the famous Zulu chief.* (NGUNI)

Sigora (m) The stout one. (NGUNI)

Sigqibokazi (f) **Sigqibo** (m) The last-born. (NGUNI)

Sigubudu (m) Strong man. (NGUNI)

Sihambi (m) A traveller. (NGUNI)

Sihlangusabayeni The shield of the in-laws. *Traditional folktale name.* (NGUNI)

Sihle Short form of 'Siphesihle', 'Siphiwengesihle'. (NGUNI)

Sihlobo A relation. (NGUNI)

Sijabulisiwe (f) We have been made to rejoice. (NGUNI)

Sikelela Bless. (NGUNI)

Sikhulile We have grown. (NGUNI)

Sikhulule (m) Free us. (NGUNI)

Sikhulumi (m) The speaker. *Traditional folktale name.* (NGUNI)

Sikumbuzo **Sikhumbuzo** (m) A keepsake; remembrance. (NGUNI)

Sikwiza (f) Sister-in-law. (NGUNI)

Silaqalaqa (m) One with a guilty conscience. (NGUNI)

Silindokuhle We are expecting what is good. (NGUNI)

Silindubuhle We are expecting goodness. (NGUNI)

Silomo The famous one. (NGUNI)

Silulami Recovered. (NGUNI)

Silungile (f) Good and kind. (NGUNI)

Silwane (m) An animal. *Protective name* (NGUNI)

Simamile (f) The stable one. (NGUNI)

Simanga Simangaliso A miracle. (NGUNI)

Simangele We have been surprised. *Name may be given for an unexpected pregnancy.* (NGUNI)

Simbongile (f) We are grateful. (NGUNI)

Simemo An invitation. (NGUNI)

Similo One's character. (NGUNI)

Similonhle Steadfast; unswerving character. (NGUNI)

Simiso Simo (m) This is what is expected of us. (NGUNI)

Simnikiwe (f) This child has been handed to us. (NGUNI)

Simomondiya (f) Plump and healthy one. (NGUNI)

Simphiwe Simpiwe Our gift. (NGUNI)

Simunye We are one. (NGUNI)

Simxolele We have forgiven. *This name could be given in a situation where the mother was defiled.* (NGUNI)

Sinabo We have them. (NGUNI)

Sinakekelwe Taken care of. (NGUNI)

Sinalo We have. (NGUNI)

Sincobile (f) We have conquered. (NGUNI)

Sindile (f) Recovered; saved. (NGUNI)

Sindisiwe Sindi Sindiswa (f) Saved; redeemed. (NGUNI)

Sindzisani Force him to recognize this child as his. *Name given when the father refuses to accept the pregnancy.* (XITSONGA)

Sinegugu Sine (f) We have a treasure. (NGUNI)

Sinenhlanhla (f) We are the lucky ones. (NGUNI)

Sinenkosi The Lord is on our side. (NGUNI)

Sinentobeko We have respect. (NGUNI)

Sinephuti A hairy one. (NGUNI)

Sinethemba We have hope. (NGUNI)

Sinetjhudu We are fortunate. (NGUNI)

Singani A lover. (NGUNI)

Singathwa One who is safely protected. (NGUNI)

Sinhle (f) It is good. (NGUNI)

Sino (f) Short form for any of the following 'Sinothile', 'Sinoxolo', 'Sinothando', 'Sinomusa'. (NGUNI)

Sinolwazi (f) We are knowledgeable. (NGUNI)

Sinomusa (f) We have grace. (NGUNI)

Sinomzi (f) We have a home. (NGUNI)

Sinothando (f) We have love. (NGUNI)

Sinothile (f) We are wealthy. (NGUNI)

Sinovuyo (f) We have joy. (NGUNI)

Sinoxolo (f) We have peace; we are pardoned. (NGUNI)

Sintu Tradition. (NGUNI)

Sipha Short form of 'Siphamandla'. (NGUNI)

Siphalaphala (f) An attractive one with a fair complexion. (NGUNI)

Siphamandla (m) Give us strength. (NGUNI)

Siphathisiwe (f) God has assisted us. (NGUNI)

Siphatho Caring. (NGUNI)

Siphekuthula We are carrying peace. (NGUNI)

Siphelele We are now complete. (NGUNI)

Siphenkosi Give us, Lord. (NGUNI)

Siphephelo Refuge; shelter. (NGUNI)

Siphephile We are safe. (NGUNI)

Siphesihle **Siphe** Good gift. *A combination of 'Sipho' and 'Esihle'.* (NGUNI)

Siphetfo Conclusively; for good. *Name given to the last-born child.* (NGUNI)

Siphindiwe Has been repeated. (NGUNI)

Siphiwayena We are being given this one. (NGUNI)

Siphiwe (f) We have been given. (NGUNI)

Siphiwengesihle (f) We have kindly received. (NGUNI)

Siphiwengomusa (f) We have graciously received. (NGUNI)

Siphiwinhlanhla (f) We have been blessed. (NGUNI)

Siphiwo *See 'Sipho'.* (NGUNI)

Siphiwosenkosi God's gift. (NGUNI)

Siphiwosethu Our gift. (NGUNI)

Siphiwumusa We have been graced. (NGUNI)

Siphiwuthando We have been given love. (NGUNI)

Sipho Sipo (f) Gift. (NGUNI)

Sipokazi Siphokazi (f) A Great gift. *Kazi is a feminizing suffix.* (NGUNI)

Siphosethu Our gift. (NGUNI)

Siphumle We have rested. (NGUNI)

Sipumze Relieve us. (NGUNI)

Siqamulamayezi (f) One who breaks the clouds. *Praise name for the one whose beauty can make a cloudy day sunny.* (NGUNI)

Siqinisile (f) We are truthful. (NGUNI)

Siqondile (f) We are straight. (NGUNI)

Sisa (f) The merciful one. (NGUNI)

Sisanda (f) We are still increasing. (NGUNI)

Sisasenkosi (f) God's mercy. (NGUNI)

Sisekelo A foundation. (NGUNI)

Sisimoga Respect. (SOTHO)

Sisipho It's a gift. (NGUNI)

Sisiphokazi (f) This is a great gift. (NGUNI)

Sisiwe (f) Has been lent to us. (NGUNI)

Sisonke We are together. (NGUNI)

Sitandiwe We are loved. (NGUNI)

Sitfunywa Messenger. (NGUNI)

Sithabile (f) We are happy. (NGUNI)

Sithabiso One making us happy. (NGUNI)

Sithabiso Our joy. (NGUNI)

Sithandwa Lovely one. (NGUNI)

Sithelo Fruit. (NGUNI)

Sithelwesihle Good produce. (NGUNI)

Sithembele We are hopeful. (NGUNI)

Sithembile (f) We are hopeful. (NGUNI)

Sithembiso Sithe (m) Promise. (NGUNI)

Sitheni What have we said? *Usually when the community suspected that someone was pregnant.* (NGUNI)

Sithethi The eloquent speaker. (NGUNI)

Sithokozile (f) We are happy. (NGUNI)

Sithuli A quiet one. (NGUNI)

Sithunzi (m) Dignified one. (NGUNI)

Sitsandzile (f) We have loved. (NGUNI)

Sitsembiso Promise. (NGUNI)

Sive Hear us. (NGUNI)

Sivhada Sivhi Peace. (TSHIVENDA)

Sivhutomu Sivhu Life. (XITSONGA)

Siviwe God has heard us. (NGUNI)

Siviya (m) Name of a former Botswana chief. (SOTHO)

Sivukile We have been reawakened. (NGUNI)

Sivumelwano Agreement. (NGUNI)

Sivuyile We are joyful. (NGUNI)

Sivuyiseni Rejoice with us. (NGUNI)

Sivuyisiwe We are rejoicing. (NGUNI)

Siwelile Siwe We have crossed over. (NGUNI)

Sixhoshiwe Something has entered your eyes and disturbed the view. *This expression is used to refer to someone who has lost focus. Such a name can be given in the case of a teenage pregnancy.* (NGUNI)

Sixolile We have forgiven. (NGUNI)

Sixolisiwe (f) We have reconciled. (NGUNI)

Siyabonga Siya We are thankful. (NGUNI)

Siyabulela We are grateful. (NGUNI)

Siyakhula We are growing. (NGUNI)

Siyambonga We praise him. (NGUNI)

Siyamcela We are asking for him. (NGUNI)

Siyamthanda We love the child. (NGUNI)

Siyamyaleza We are sending him as a messenger. (NGUNI)

Siyanda We are increasing. (NGUNI)

Siyasanga We have been awarded. (NGUNI)

Siyathemba Siyatemba We are trusting. (NGUNI)

Siza Sizani Helper. (NGUNI)

Sizeka Sizekani Allow to be helped. (NGUNI)

Siziwe One who has been helped. (NGUNI)

Sizolwethu This is our help. *A child can be looked upon as an economic stabilizer in an African home setting.* (NGUNI)

Sizophila We will live. (NGUNI)

Sizwe (m) You are a nation. (NGUNI)

Sizwile (m) We have heard. (NGUNI)

Skhakhameli (m) A dignified person. (NGUNI)

Skhumbuzo (m) *See 'Skumbuzo'.*

Skoni (f) My sister-in-law. (NGUNI)

Skukuza He who sweeps clean. (XITSONGA)

Skumbuzo (m) A reminder. *Name given to commemorate a person or an event* (NGUNI)

Slindzile (f) *See 'Lindile'.*

Smangele Sma (f) We are amazed. (NGUNI)

Snakekelo Caring one. (NGUNI)

Snazo (f) We have them. *This name will be given where there are lots of girls in the family.* (NGUNI)

Sodolo (m) A person strong in character. (NGUNI)

Sofonia (m) The Lord is my secret. *Sotho name of biblical origin, derived from Zephaniah.* (SOTHO)

Solakhe (m) His eye. (NGUNI)

Solani (m) What are you suspecting? (NGUNI) (TSONGA)

Solenkosi (m) The eye of the king. *Name for the royal representative.* (NGUNI)

Solofela (f) One bringing hope. (SOTHO)

Solofetsa (f) Promise. (SOTHO)

Solomzi (m) Watching after the home. *Literally the eye of the home.* (NGUNI)

Solule (m) Extend the family. (NGUNI)

Solulele (m) Stretch us. (NGUNI)

Somelezo (m) Encouragement. (NGUNI)

Somizi (m) One who has authority over the homesteads. (NGUNI)

Sompisi (m) Of the Hyena. *Usually used in folktales.* (NGUNI)

Sompiyezwe (m) Father of the World War. *Name given to one born during either World War.* (NGUNI)

Sondonzima (m) Hard wheel. *This name has connotations of hardship. Traditional folktale name.* (NGUNI)

Sonele (m) We are adequate. (NGUNI)

Soneni (m) What wrong have we done? *Name employed as a communicative strategy.* (NGUNI)

Songezile (m) We have added. (NGUNI)

Songezo (m) The additional one. (NGUNI)

Songezwa (m) An additional one. (NGUNI)

Sonosakhe (m) It is his sin. *Such a name was used by the grandmother to accuse the boy who impregnated her teenage daughter.* (NGUNI)

Sonto (f) Sunday. *Name given to a child born on Sunday.* (NGUNI)

Sonwabile (f) We are comfortable. (NGUNI)

Sonwabo **Sonwabiso** (m) One who brings comfort and ease. (NGUNI)

Sowethu (m) One who belongs to us. (NGUNI)

Soxolo (m) One bringing reconciliation. (NGUNI)

Sphamandla S'phamandla Spha (m) God we ask for strength. (NGUNI)

Sphenge (f) A healthy and diligent girl. (NGUNI)

Sphesihle (f) A beautiful gift. (NGUNI)

Sphetfo (m) The end. *Given to the last-born child.* (NGUNI)

Sphikelele (m) We are adamant. (NGUNI)

Sphokazi (f) The great gift. (NGUNI)

Sphosenkosi (m) Our gift from the Lord. (NGUNI)

Sposakhe (m) His or her gift. (NGUNI)

Stemere (m) One born in September. (NGUNI)

Sthandiwe (m) We are loved. (NGUNI)

Sthembele Sthe (m) We are hoping. (NGUNI)

Sthembile (f) We are hopeful. (NGUNI)

Sthembiso (m) Promise. (NGUNI)

Suhla (m) Penetrate. *Giving birth may be the way the mother will be able to penetrate the heart of her in-laws and be accepted as one of them.* (NGUNI)

Suka-ka-tiko (m) Leave the country. *The child was born and the family was chased away from the farm where they used to work.* (XITSONGA)

Sunguti (m) January. *Name can be given to a child born in January.* (XITSONGA)

Swa-ku-fanyana (m) That which dies little by little. (XITSONGA)

Swarela Forgive. (SOTHO)

Swelabatsheli Lacking advisors. (NGUNI)

Swinene Well or good. (XITSONGA)

Swivuriso Proverbs. (XITSONGA)

Tabisa (f) Causing one to rejoice. (SOTHO)

Taga (f) Shine. (SOTHO)

Tagafatsa (f) Cause to shine. (SOTHO)

Tagilego (f) Shining; bright. (SOTHO)

Takadiyi How are we doing? *The name-giver is using this name to inform others that they are doing well.* (XITSONGA)

Takalane Happy. (TSHIVENDA)

Takalani Taki Be happy; rejoice. (TSHIVENDA)

Takangwane (f) The girl born is of the Ngwane clan in Swaziland. (NGUNI)

Tanana Come. (XITSONGA)

Tana-na-mi-swi-tiva (m) Come prepared. (XITSONGA)

Tandaza Pray. *Name used when the parents believe that the child was obtained through prayer.* (NGUNI)

Tandekile (f) Beloved one. (NGUNI)

Tandi (f) Short form of 'Tandile', 'Tandiwe'. (NGUNI)

Tandile (f) One who loves. (NGUNI)

Tandiwe (f) The beloved. (NGUNI)

Tando Love. (NGUNI)

Tandokazi (f) Great love. (NGUNI)

Tandose (f) The lucky one. (NGUNI)

Tandzile (f) Have loved. (NGUNI)

Tanganya Tanga To add. (TSHIVENDA)

Tangeni Let us give praise. (TSHIVENDA)

Tankiso Gratitude. *Having miscarried before, the parents are grateful to finally give birth.* (XITSONGA)

Tapologo Relaxation. (SOTHO)

Tapologô Rest; recuperate; recover. (SOTHO)

Tatana (m) Father. (XITSONGA)

Tate (m) Father. (SOTHO)

Tau (m) Lion (a clan name); one with strength and fierceness. (SOTHO)

Tebatjo (m) Made us forget the pain. (SOTHO)

Tebatso (m) Distraction; make forget. (SOTHO)

Tebello (m) Expectation. (SOTHO)

Tebogo (m) Thanksgiving. (SOTHO)

Teboho (m) Gratitude. (SOTHO)

Tefo (m) Payment; reward. (SOTHO)

Tekano (m) Sufficient. (SOTHO)

Telakufa (m) Came to die. *Name given after successive infant deaths in the family.* (XITSONGA)

Temagcino (f) The last-born one. (NGUNI)

Temalangeni (f) Of the Dlamini family. (NGUNI)

Temaswati (f) Of the Swazis. (NGUNI)

Temba (m) Trust. (NGUNI)

Tembakazi (f) Great hope. (NGUNI)

Tembeka (f) The trustworthy one. (NGUNI)

Tembela (f) Trusting in someone or something. (NGUNI)

Tembelani You must trust in. (NGUNI)

Tembile Trusting. (NGUNI)

Tembisa Promise. (NGUNI)

Temlandzo (f) Historic one. (NGUNI)

Tenanile (f) They are happy. (NGUNI)

Tendani (m) Believe. (TSHIVENDA)

Tendi (m) Believe. *From 'Thendo' (Faith).* (TSHIVENDA)

Tenele (f) They are enough. (NGUNI)

Tengetile (f) They have added on. (NGUNI)

Tfobile (f) Humbled one. (NGUNI)

Tfobisile (f) One who is modest. (NGUNI)

Tfolakele (f) One who has been found. *When the parents were looking for a girl child.* (NGUNI)

Tfolinhlanhla (f) One who has obtained luck. (NGUNI)

Thaba (m) Be glad; rejoice; be cheerful; be happy. (SOTHO)

Thaba (m) Mountain. *Usually symbolic of authority.* (SOTHO)

Thabang (m) Be happy. (SOTHO)

Thabani (m) Be happy. (NGUNI)

Thabelo (m) Prayer. (TSHIVENDA)

Thabethule (m) The one who rejoices quietly. (NGUNI)

Thabisa Thabi *See 'Thabisile'.* (NGUNI)

Thabisile (f) Happy. (NGUNI)

Thabiso (m) Joy-bringer. (SOTHO)

Thabizolo (m) The one who rejoiced in the past. (NGUNI)

Thabo (m)   Happiness. (SOTHO)

Thabsile (f)   The happy. (NGUNI)

Thakasile (f)   The excited one. (NGUNI)

Thakgalo   Joy; happiness. (SOTHO)

Thakgega   Prosper; turn out well. (SOTHO)

Thami   A short form of 'Thamsanqa'. (NGUNI)

Thamsanqa (m)   Luck. (NGUNI)

Thamsanqelisa (f)   Cause to confer a favour. (NGUNI)

Thanda   Love. (NGUNI)

Thandabantu   The one who loves people. (NGUNI)

Thandaza   Pray. (NGUNI)

Thandazile (f)   She has prayed. (NGUNI)

Thandazwa   Thandazo (f)   Pray. (NGUNI)

Thandeka (f)   Lovely. (NGUNI)

Thandekile (f)   The loved one. (NGUNI)

Thandile   Thandi (f)   Loved. (NGUNI)

Thandisizwe (m)   Lover of the nation. *Usually royals will have names associated with their commitment to the nation.* (NGUNI)

Thandiswa (f)   One with affectionate feelings. (NGUNI)

Thandiwe (f)   Beloved. (NGUNI)

Thandizwe   One who loves worldly pleasure. (NGUNI)

Thando   *See 'Tando'.* (NGUNI)

Thandokazi (f)   One who is cherished above all others. (NGUNI)

Thandokuhle Be keen on what is good. (NGUNI)
Thandolwakhe His love. (NGUNI)
Thandolwethu Our Love. (NGUNI)
Thandubuhle Lover of beauty. (NGUNI)
Thandukukhanya Lover of light. (NGUNI)
Thandukwazi Keen to know. (NGUNI)
Thandunina The one who loves the mother. (NGUNI)
Thanduxolo The peace lover. (NGUNI)
Thanduyise The one devoted to the father. (NGUNI)
Thangithini What am I to say? *This name is a response to an ongoing dialogue in the family.* (NGUNI)
Thantaswa One carried in a palm of a hand. (NGUNI)
Thanyani Be wise and careful. *Name was given to warn the child about those who may want to do him harm.* (TSHIVENDA)
Thapeli Appeal. (SOTHO)
Thapelo Thapi Prayer; plea. (SOTHO)
Thatayaone (f) His (God's) strength. (SOTHO)
Thathani (f) Take her. *Name will be given to encourage the father to marry the mother.* (NGUNI)
Thathelwani (f) Why are you taking her? *Grandmother was not in approval of the wife her son had chosen.* (NGUNI)
Thathiwe (f) Has been taken. *The birth of the child coincided with the mother's marriage and the name served as a memorial of the wedding.* (NGUNI)

Thathwaphi (f) Where did you get her? *Through this name, the mother in-law was venting her disapproval of her daughter-in-law, asking where did her son get this woman?* (NGUNI)

Thato Will; desire. (SOTHO)

Thavha (m) Mountain. *Usually symbolic of authority.* (TSHIVENDA)

Thavhayamipfa (m) Thorny mountain. (TSHIVENDA)

Thebe (m) A shield. *Symbol of protection.* (SOTHO)

Thekga (m) Support. (SOTHO)

Thekge (m) Must support. (SOTHO)

Thelenyane (m) Leader; champion. (SOTHO)

Thelile (f) Fruitful. (NGUNI)

Thelumusa The one who pours out grace. (NGUNI)

Themba (m) Hope. (NGUNI)

Thembakazi Great hope. (NGUNI)

Thembalethu Our hope. (NGUNI)

Thembalihle Good hope. (NGUNI)

Thembeka (f) Trustworthy. (NGUNI)

Thembekile (f) Trusted. (NGUNI)

Thembela (f) Trust in. (NGUNI)

Thembelani (m) *See 'Thembela'.*

Thembeletsheni (m) Trust the stone. *Advising against putting trust in men. Traditional folktale name.* (NGUNI)

Thembelihle (f) Good hope. (NGUNI)

Thembeni (f) Where is your trust? (NGUNI)

Thembile (f) One who is hopeful. (NGUNI)

Thembinkosi (m) Trust in the Lord. (NGUNI)

Thembisa (f) Promise. *See 'Thembisile'.* (NGUNI)

Thembisile (f) She has promised. (NGUNI)

Thendo (m) Faith. (TSHIVENDA)

Thenjiwe (f) One who is trusted. (NGUNI)

Thereso Truth; veracity; reality; truism. (SOTHO)

Thethekgetsa Support; prop up; sustain. (SOTHO)

Thiambi A short form of 'Athiambiwi'. (TSHIVENDA)

Thiathu Short form of 'Athiathu'. (TSHIVENDA)

Thifhelimbilu Short form of 'Athifhelimbilu'. (TSHIVENDA)

Thihi One. (TSHIVENDA)

Thikhathali Short form of 'Athikhathali'. (TSHIVENDA)

Thilivhali Short form of 'Athilivhali'; one who does not forget . (TSHIVENDA)

Thimangali Short form of 'Athimangali'. (TSHIVENDA)

Thinandavha Thina (f) Short form of 'Athinandavha'. (TSHIVENDA)

Thinavhudzulo (f) I have nowhere to stay. *The name is a communication about an ongoing situation.* (TSHIVENDA)

Thinawanga (f) I have nobody. *The name is a communication about an ongoing situation.* (TSHIVENDA)

Thirani Work. (XITSONGA)

Thlawuliriwa Thlawu The chosen one. (XITSONGA)

Thobani Be humbled. (NGUNI)

Thobekile The submissive and obedient one. (NGUNI)

Thobela Humbled. (NGUNI)

Thobile Thobi The humbled one. (NGUNI)

Thohoyandou (m) Head of an elephant. *First name of a historical chief of the Vha Venda nation.* (TSHIVENDA)

Thoko Thokozile (f) Rejoiced. (NGUNI)

Thokulula Enlarge. (NGUNI)

Tholakele (f) She has been found. (NGUNI)

Tholindawo One who has found a place. (NGUNI)

Tholinhlanhla We have found good fortune. (NGUNI)

Tholithemba We have found hope. (NGUNI)

Tholiwe *See 'Tholakele'.* (NGUNI)

Tholumusa Found grace. (NGUNI)

Tholumuzi I have found a home. (NGUNI)

Thomololo A pleasant person. (NGUNI)

Thoriso Praise. (SOTHO)

Thotobolo (m) Place for dumping rubbish or refuse. *Protective name used after successive infant deaths in the family.* (SOTHO)

Thovhela (m) Venda chief. (TSHIVENDA)

Thozama Thozile Thozamile (m) The humble one. (NGUNI)

Thubalakhe It is her opportunity. *Giving birth may signify a breakthrough in the mother's status in her marital home.* (NGUNI)

Thubalami It's my turn. (NGUNI)

Thubalethu It is our chance. (NGUNI)

Thubelihle A good opportunity. (NGUNI)

Thulani Be quiet; be at peace. *The birth of the child has ended idle talk or gossip.* (NGUNI)

Thulasizwe Let the nation be at peace. (NGUNI)

Thulawazi Be still and know. *Ending of the struggle to conceive a child.* (NGUNI)

Thulebona The one who keeps quiet whilst still seeing. (NGUNI)

Thuletu Completely quiet. (NGUNI)

Thulisa (f) See 'Thulani'.

Thulisile Thuli Thulisiwe (f) One who is behaving themselves quietly. (NGUNI)

Thumelo God-sent. (NGUNI)

Thunjana Small intestine. *A name given to the last-born.* (XITSONGA)

Thupela Be beautiful. (SOTHO)

Thuso Assisted; helped. (SOTHO)

Thuthuka Progress. *Birth of a child reflects a progress in social status.* (NGUNI)

Thuthukani You must progress. (NGUNI)

Thuthukile (f) The one who has progressed. (NGUNI)

Thuthuzela (f) To console. *As in singing a lullaby.* (NGUNI)

Thuto Lesson. (SOTHO)

Tibombisa (f) Adorning self. (XITSONGA)

Tibuyile (f) They have come back. *The cows which were used to pay the bridal price have come back through the birth of the child.* (NGUNI)

Tichawoma We shall see. (TSHIVENDA)

Tiegosetsano Tiego (m) Delay; procrastinate. (SOTHO)

Tiisetso One who perseveres. (SOTHO)

Tilweni Heaven. (XITSONGA)

Timisa Be courageous. (XITSONGA)

Timotia (m) Honour of God; valued of God. *Sotho name of biblical origin, derived from Timothy.* (SOTHO)

Tinhle (f) They are beautiful. (NGUNI)

Tintswalo Motherly love, kindness or mercy. (XITSONGA)

Tinyiko Gifts. (XITSONGA)

Titshere Teacher. (SOTHO)

Titundulume One of good reputation. (XITSONGA)

Tivamile (f) They are frequent. *Usually given where there are lots of girls in the family.* (NGUNI)

Tivani (m) Knowledge. (XITSONGA)

Tiyani (m) Be strong; firm up. (XITSONGA)

Tiyimiseni (m) Steady up. (XITSONGA)

Tiyiseka (m) Persevere. (XITSONGA)

Tiyiselane (m) Hold on. (XITSONGA)

Tjhudu (m) Luck. (NGUNI)

Tlabakela (m) Rest. (SOTHO)

Tladi Lightning. *Born on a day when there was thunder and lightning.* (SOTHO)

Tlakula One carried in the arms. (XITSONGA)

Tlakusa Pull up. (XITSONGA)

Tlali Has been fulfilled. (SOTHO)

Tlangelani (m) Celebrate. (XITSONGA)

Tlhalalo Joy; rejoicing. (SOTHO)

Tlhalefo Wisdom; knowledge. (SOTHO)

Tlhallelo Announcement. (SOTHO)

Tlhaloganyo Understanding; comprehension. (SOTHO)

Tlhamaganya Help to repair. (SOTHO)

Tlhanoga Person who changes his mind. *The name was used by the mother as a communication strategy to the father.* (SOTHO)

Tlhantlhamisute Following upon false hopes of pregnancy. *'Swiute' means the period during which a woman may miss her menstrual period without being pregnant. In this case a child was conceived after such a period.* (XITSONGA)

Tlhaologanyo (m) Notion. (SOTHO)

Tlharihani (m) Get wise. (XITSONGA)

Tlhatloga (m) Lift up. (SOTHO)

Tlhatlolagana (m) Follow one another. (SOTHO)

Tlhelani (m) Go back. *Name given if it is believed that the name-bearer brought misfortune.* (XITSONGA)

Tlhokomela (m) Prudent. (SOTHO)

Tlhokomelo (f) Being careful. (SOTHO)

Tlholo (f) Victory. (SOTHO)

Tlhomamiso (f) Confirmation. (SOTHO)

Tlhomogelo   Tlhomogi (f) Compassion; mercy. (SOTHO)

Tlhopha (f) Choose; select. (SOTHO)

Tlhotlhwa (f) Price. (SOTHO)

Tlhotse (f) Created; made. (SOTHO)

Tlhweko (f) Purity. (SOTHO)

Tlotla (m) Praise. (SOTHO)

Tlotliso (m) Honoured one. (SOTHO)

Tlotlo (m) Honour. (SOTHO)

Tlotlomela (m) Be exalted. (SOTHO)

Tlou (m) Elephant. (SOTHO)

Tobani (m) *See 'Thobani'.*

Tobeka (f) Be obedient. (NGUNI)

Todi (m) Short form of 'Ntodeni'. (TSHIVENDA)

Toko (f) Short form of 'Tokozile'. (NGUNI)

Tokoloho Freedom; independence. (SOTHO)

Tokozani (m) Be happy. (NGUNI)

Tonoga Be exposed. (SOTHO)

Topollo Emancipation; release. (SOTHO)

Tozie (f) *See 'Thozamile'.*

Tsakane (f) Happiness. (XITSONGA)

Tsakani Be joyful; gladness. (XITSONGA)

Tsame Mine. (SOTHO)

Tsandziwe (f) *See 'Sitsandzile'.*

Tsavutsavu The one who pulls out water. (XITSONGA)

Tsebo (m) Knowledge. (SOTHO)

T'sehla (m) Yellow man. *Meaning lion's cub.* (SOTHO)

Tsela (m) Pathway. (SOTHO)

Tseliso Tshediso (m) Consolation. (SOTHO)

Tsembekile (f) Faithful one. (NGUNI)

Tsembeying What do you expect from your actions? Why are you behaving like that? *This name would be used as a communicative strategy in an ongoing dialogue.* (XITSONGA)

Tsepiso (m) Promise. (SOTHO)

Tsepo (m) Hope. (SOTHO)

Tshakalati They hate me. *This name is used by the wife of a polygamist, who is despised by her husband and his other wives.* (XITSONGA)

Tshamano (m) One with wisdom. (TSHIVENDA)

Tshameleni (m) What is the good of staying? *Such a name was used as a communication strategy by the ill-treated mother at the husband's home.* (XITSONGA)

Tshamisa (m) Establish. (XITSONGA)

Tshanduko (m) Change. *Noun form of 'Shandukani'.* (TSHIVENDA)

Tshavutha (m) An enthusiast. (NGUNI)

Tshawe (m) One of high rank; a prince or royal chief. (NGUNI)

Tshedisega Be consoled. (SOTHO)

Tshego Laughter. (SOTHO)

Tshegofatso Grace; blessing. (SOTHO)

Tshemba (m) Trust. (XITSONGA)

Tshembani Trust. (XITSONGA)

Tshenge Short form of 'Ntshengedzeni'. (TSHIVENDA)

Tshenolo Revelation; someone who has gone beyond expectations, usually in a bad way. (SOTHO)

Tshephang Keep trusting. (SOTHO)

Tshepiso (m) A promise. (SOTHO)

Tshepo (m) To have faith and hope. (SOTHO)

Tshiananeo A tale; an event. *Usually a bad one.* (TSHIVENDA)

Tshidino Something that bothers someone. *Name given to protect the bearer from evil spirits.* (TSHIVENDA)

Tshifanyiso Portrait. (TSHIVENDA)

Tshifhiwa (f) Gift. (TSHIVENDA)

Tshiisaphungo (f) One who spreads gossip. *Normally this name would be chosen when there is a suspicion that someone in the family is spreading misinformation about the family.* (TSHIVENDA)

Tshikaro (f) Carrying. (SOTHO)

Tshikhuma (f) Be abundant. (SOTHO)

Tshilidzi (f) Mercy. (TSHIVENDA)

Tshililo (f) Weeping; lamentation. (TSHIVENDA)

Tshimangadzo (f) Miracle; something that is amazing; a great surprise. (TSHIVENDA)

Tshinakaho Something cute/charming. *Derived from the Tshivenda proverb 'Tshinakaho a tshi yi thambo, tshi no ya thambo ndi mutshinyal': meaning that something so beautiful cannot last forever.* (TSHIVENDA)

Tshinyadzo Tshinya Disrespect. *Name-giver may be feeling disrespected and will then use the name to register the complaint politely.* (TSHIVENDA)

Tshinyalani Be damned. *This name is used to give the impression that the child is not wanted with the hope that this is enough to protect the child against the jealous spirit.* (TSHIVENDA)

Tshio Victory. (SOTHO)

Tshivhase One who burns other people's homesteads. *Name derived from the praise poem for a warrior.* (TSHIVENDA)

Tshiwandalani One born during drought or famine. (TSHIVENDA)

Tshiya Pillar. (SOTHO)

Tshoganyetso (f) Unexpected. (SOTHO)

Tsholofelo (f) Hope; expectation. (SOTHO)

Tshonisile (f) The one who has caused great loss. *Teenage pregnancy can be regarded as a great loss for parents who have invested so much in their daughter, hoping for economic returns.* (NGUNI)

Tshuana An orphan. (SOTHO)

Tshwaraganang Be united. (NGUNI)

Tshwene (m) Baboon. *Protective name which is replaced by a proper name after initiation.* (SOTHO)

Tsietsi (m) Confusion; predicament. (SOTHO)

Tsikitla Tickle. (SOTHO)

Tsireledzo Protection. (TSHIVENDA)

Tsoeu The one who is fair-skinned. (SOTHO)

Tsoga (m) Rise. (SOTHO)

Tsoha (m) Rise up. (SOTHO)

Tsokombela (f) Sweet one. (XITSONGA)

Tsua (m) Pronounce judgement upon. (SOTHO)

Tsumbezo (m) Set an example. (TSHIVENDA)

Tsumbi (m) Short form for 'Tsumbezo'. (TSHIVENDA)

Tsumbo (m) Example. (TSHIVENDA)

Tsundzukani (m) Remember. (XITSONGA)

Tsundzuxa (m) Advise. (XITSONGA)

Tsuntsukani Remembered. (XITSONGA)

Tswani (f) Short form of 'Ditswanelo'. (SOTHO)

Tsweu The fair one. (SOTHO)

Tuelo Payment. (SOTHO)

Tukisi (m) He who solves or attends to problems. (SOTHO)

Tulani *See 'Thulani'.* (NGUNI)

Tuma Become known/famous. (SOTHO)

Tumeka The obedient messenger. (NGUNI)

Tumêlanô Accord; agreement. (SOTHO)

Tumelo Believe. (SOTHO)

Tumi Short form of 'Tumelo', 'Tumile'. (SOTHO)

Tumile Be renowned. (SOTHO)

Tumilego One who is renowned. (SOTHO)

Tumisa (f) Make known. (SOTHO)

Tumisang (f) Give praises. (SOTHO)

Tumisho (f) Praises. (XITSONGA)

Tumiso (f) Praise. (SOTHO)

Tungu Short form of 'Ntungufhadzeni'. (TSHIVENDA)

Tunwana Cisticola bird. *Name given for a child who is very small at birth.* (SOTHO)

Tusekile One who is praiseworthy. (NGUNI)
Tutani You must leave this place. (NGUNI)
Twanano Unity. (XITSONGA)
Txintxase One who changes easily. (NGUNI)

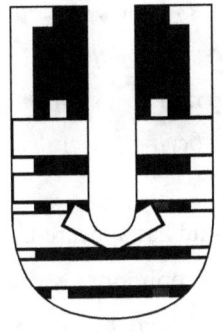

Umhlobo The friendly one. (NGUNI)

Uminathi He (God) is standing with us. (NGUNI)

Unarine God is always with us. (TSHIVENDA)

Unathi Unati He is with us. *This name is in accord with the belief that children are a gift from God.* (NGUNI)

Uvatera God help us. *Parents may be going through a situation which is difficult at the birth of this child.* (TSHIVENDA)

Uvelile (m) The child has appeared. (NGUNI)

Uvolwethu (m) Our opinion. *The family did not initially approve of the parents' relationship; through getting the child the couple are validating their relationship.* (NGUNI)

Uzothile (m) The humbled one. (NGUNI)

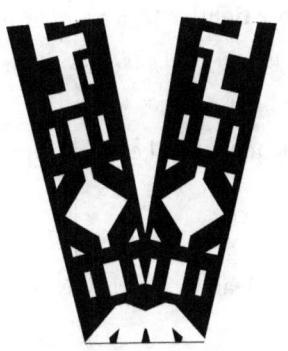

Vakelo Gain. *The birth of a child is considered a gain for the family.* (XITSONGA)

Vali (f) Short form of 'Valisisa'. (NGUNI)

Valisisa (f) Close tightly. *Advice for the mother to be sterilised since she kept giving birth whilst the family had no resources to look after them.* (NGUNI)

Vamuhle Someone who likes to do wonderful things. (NGUNI)

Vanhu People. (XITSONGA)

Vanhu-mavele Mealies. *The child is as necessary as the food.* (XITSONGA)

Vata Showing unhappiness. (XITSONGA)

Vatiswa (f) One who is adorned. (NGUNI)

Vela Appear. (NGUNI)

Velangesihle Has appeared by grace. *Parents have been waiting for the birth of this child for a long time.* (NGUNI)

Velaphi **Velephi** (m) Where from? *Name given when the mother has not publicly declared who the father is. She might have not been involved in any open relationship or the husband has been away from home for quite some time.* (NGUNI)

Velenkosini (m) The one who has come from the Lord. (NGUNI)

Velethu (m) Our land. *This name is a communication strategy with regard to a dispute over land.* (NGUNI)

Velile The child has appeared. (NGUNI)

Veliswa (f) Created. (NGUNI)

Velwano Compassionate one. (NGUNI)

Vhahangwele Forgive them. (TSHIVENDA)

Vhakoma (m) Chief's messenger. (TSHIVENDA)

Vhamusanda (m) Headman; chief. (TSHIVENDA)

Vhanga (m) Of me. (TSHIVENDA)

Vhatedzani Embrace. (TSHIVENDA)

Vhengani (m) Hate it. (TSHIVENDA)

Vho This is a Venda title of respect, mostly prefixed to the name and/or the surname. (TSHIVENDA)

Vhonani See; perceive. (TSHIVENDA)

Vhoniswani Has been made to perceive. (TSHIVENDA)

Vhudifari Self control. (TSHIVENDA)

Vhudifhimi Self-conscious. (TSHIVENDA)

Vhudifulufheli Self-confidence. (TSHIVENDA)

Vhudipileli Self-defence. (TSHIVENDA)

Vhudivhuedzi Humility. (TSHIVENDA)

Vhudivhusi Self-government. (TSHIVENDA)

Vhudza Tell. *Giving a name is always a chance to tell a story or to register a complaint.* (TSHIVENDA)

Vhugedi Comfort. (TSHIVENDA)

Vhuhali Courage. (TSHIVENDA)

Vhuhosi (m) Chieftaincy. (TSHIVENDA)

Vhuhwavho Kindness. (TSHIVENDA)

Vhukondeleli Perseverance. (TSHIVENDA)

Vhukosi (m) Royalty. (XITSONGA)

Vhulahani (m) Kill. *Name-giver will dare their enemies to go ahead with their harmful intention.* (TSHIVENDA)

Vhulenda (m) Gentleness. (TSHIVENDA)

Vhumula Rested. (XITSONGA)

Vhunaki Charm. (TSHIVENDA)

Vhunzhi Great number. (TSHIVENDA)

Vhupfumedzanyi Reconciliation. (TSHIVENDA)

Vhuphulusi Deliverance. (TSHIVENDA)

Vhusani Vhusa (m) Rule over; reign. (TSHIVENDA)

Vhushaka (m) Blood relationship. (TSHIVENDA)

Vhushavhelo (m) Refuge. (TSHIVENDA)

Vhushumesi (m) Diligence. (TSHIVENDA)

Vhusifhelembilu Patience. (TSHIVENDA)

Vhutali Wisdom. (TSHIVENDA)

Vhuthuhawe His kindness. *Name referring to the kindness of God for giving this child to the family.* (TSHIVENDA)

Vhutshilo Vhutsi Life. (TSHIVENDA)

Vhutshilondihawe It is His (God's) life. (TSHIVENDA)

Vikelwa One who is being shielded. (NGUNI)

Visicelo (God) Heard our request. (NGUNI)

Visiswa God has clearly heard. (NGUNI)

Viwe God has heard. (NGUNI)

Vizicelo (God) Hear our requests. (NGUNI)

Vonani You must perceive. (XITSONGA)

Vonga Give thanks. (XITSONGA)

Vongani Be thankful. (XITSONGA)

Voninga Voni Enlighten. (XITSONGA)

Vonisisa Discern. (XITSONGA)

Votelwa Been voted for. (NGUNI)

Vukani Arise. (NGUNI)

Vukatimuni (f) What type of marriage? *The mother in-law used the naming of the child to show her disapproval of her son's marriage.* (XITSONGA)

Vukayibambe (m) One who does things without any planning or order. (NGUNI)

VuKheta (m) Orderliness. (XITSONGA)

Vukhomba (m) Maturity. (XITSONGA)

Vukhosi (m) Chief or royalty. (XITSONGA)

Vukile (m) Rise; get up. (NGUNI)

Vukona (m) Presence. (XITSONGA)

Vukosi (m) Kingship. (XITSONGA)

Vukwele (f) Jealousy. *On the part of the women in a polygamous home.* (XITSONGA)

Vula Open. *Sometimes the first born is said to have opened the womb.* (NGUNI)

Vulehambilu Perserverance. (XITSONGA)

Vulindlela Make way. (NGUNI)

Vulisango Open the gate. *When the bride enters the marital home it is usually said that she is entering the gate irrespective of whether there is actually a gate or not.* (NGUNI)

Vuloyi Witchcraft. *Mother will give this name to her child when she has been accused of using witchcraft. She does this to defend herself and to dare the public opinion of the accusers.* (XITSONGA)

Vululami Righteouness. (XITSONGA)

Vumazonke (m) Someone who consents to everything. *Named for someone with a pliable character.* (NGUNI)

Vumbilu (f) Patience. (XITSONGA)

Vumelwana Agreement. (NGUNI)

Vumile Vumi (f) She has agreed. (NGUNI)

Vumisile (f) One who has caused you to accept. *The child can force the father to agree when she bears resemblance to him or his relations, forcing them to accept her as one of theirs.* (NGUNI)

Vumunhu Humanity. (XITSONGA)

Vunene Graciousness. (XITSONGA)

Vunile (f) She has reaped. *Meaning she has reaped the consequences of her actions; usually given for teenage pregnancies.* (NGUNI)

Vuntshunxeko (m) Independence. (XITSONGA)

Vunulisa (f) Garnish and adorn. (NGUNI)

Vunyiwe (f) Has been accepted. (NGUNI)

Vusani (m) Awaken something. *Usually it will be given in reference of the hope that the child will raise the family name.* (VENDA) (NGUNI)

Vuselekile (f) Has been revived. (NGUNI)

Vusimpi Vusi (m) The one who causes war. (NGUNI)

Vusinxiwa (m) Raise up the deserted homestead. (NGUNI)

Vusisizwe (m) Raise up the nation. (NGUNI)

Vusumuzi Vusumzi (m) Raise/develop the household or descendants. *Usually given for first born son.* (NGUNI)

Vutengi (f) Purity. (XITSONGA)

Vuthlari Wisdom. (XITSONGA)

Vutikhomi Self Control. (XITSONGA)

Vutisori Repentance. (XITSONGA)

Vutitsanwi Humility. (XITSONGA)

Vutivi Knowledge. (XITSONGA)

Vutomi Life. (XITSONGA)

Vutshembeki Loyalty. (XITSONGA)

Vuvuzela To sprinkle on, usually salt or medicine (muti). *Made popular by the 2010 FIFA world cup blow horn to sprinkle winning 'muti' on the team.* (NGUNI)

Vuxaka-u-ri-na-ye Friendship of the past (only). (XITSONGA)

Vuya Rejoice. (NGUNI)

Vuyani Be glad. (NGUNI)

Vuyelwa (f) Rejoice. (NGUNI)

Vuyile *See 'Vuyani'.* (NGUNI)

Vuyisa Cause joy. (NGUNI)

Vuyisanani Rejoice with each other. (NGUNI)

Vuyiseka Vuyiseko Be excited with joy. (NGUNI)

Vuyisile Cause rejoicing. (NGUNI)

Vuyiswa (f) Thrilled. (NGUNI)

Vuyo Joyous gladness. (NGUNI)

Vuyokazi Great joy. (NGUNI)

Vuyolwakhe Her joy. (NGUNI)

Vuyolwami My joy. (NGUNI)

Vuyolwethu Our joy. (NGUNI)

Wandile (m) Has increased. (NGUNI)

Wandisa (f) *See 'Andisa'.*

Wandisile (f) Caused increase. (NGUNI)

Warona Ours. (SOTHO)

Wasemzansi Of the South. (NGUNI)

Wayina The child is ours. (XITSONGA)

Wazha Arrival/birth of the awaited one. (SOTHO)

Wela   Welile To cross over. *Child-bearing represents moving from one stage of life to another.* (NGUNI)

Wele The twin. (NGUNI)

Wenzile A deed done. (NGUNI)

Wethu Ours. (NGUNI)

Winase (f) The best one. (NGUNI)

Winile   Wini (f) She has won. (NGUNI)

Wonga (m) Handsome one. (NGUNI)

Wongaletu (m) Our handsome one. (NGUNI)

Wongiwe (f) She has been preserved and is well protected. (NGUNI)

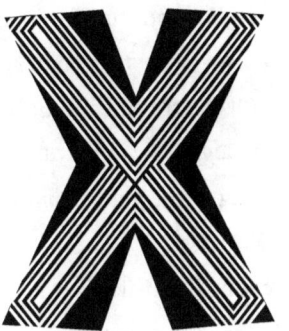

Xabisa (f) The valued one. (NGUNI)

Xabisile (f) Precious and esteemed. (NGUNI)

Xabiso Of great value. (NGUNI)

Xakekile (f) One who is confused. *Situation surrounding the birth may cause confusion to the parents.* (NGUNI)

Xamikhuva (m) Of the strange things. *One born when strange things were happening in the family.* (XITSONGA)

Xanhova (m) Thing of the veld. *Name given to an illegitimate child.* (XITSONGA)

Xhanti (m) Someone of position. (NGUNI)

Xhasoba (m) A strong supporter. (NGUNI)

Xidlodlo (m) The wax crown. *The headman used to wear a crown for authority; this child is that crown to the father.* (XITSONGA)

Xidunya (m) Stirring up. (XITSONGA)

Xidzinga (f) The wire. *This wire will be used in making bracelets.* (XITSONGA)

Xifanelo Necessity. (XITSONGA)

Xifaniso Self-portrait. (XITSONGA)

Xifuva Cause to forget. (XITSONGA)

Xigelegele (m) Traditional folktale name. (XITSONGA)

Xigodo (m) The stump. (XITSONGA)

Xihangalasi (m) The one who scatters people or things. (XITSONGA)

Xihlahleni In the bush. *Name based on the place where the mother gave birth.* (XITSONGA)

Xihlamariso Suprise. (XITSONGA)

Xihloka (m) The axe. (XITSONGA)

Xihlovo (f) A well-spring of water. (XITSONGA)

Xihungati (f) People pass their time telling stories about me. (XITSONGA)

Xikakala (m) Fearless person. (XITSONGA)

Xikhiri Suspicious behaviour. (XITSONGA)

Xikhotlawa The little bird. *Meaning a short person.* (XITSONGA)

Xikhulu The fat one. (XITSONGA)

Xikhwameni In the little basket. (XITSONGA)

Xikonwana Little locust. (XITSONGA)

Xikosi (m) Nape of the neck. *Someone who does not condescend to look at his subordinates and always shows them the nape of his neck.* (XITSONGA)

Xikundzu (m) The stump. See 'Xigodo'. (XITSONGA)

Xikuwakuwa The one who walks a special kind of gait. (XITSONGA)

Xilemanyana The little cripple. (XITSONGA)

Xilumi The one who bites. *Taken from 'Ku luma' which means 'birth pangs', the mother might have had a painful labour when giving birth to this child.* (XITSONGA)

Xiluva (f) Blossom like a flower. (XITSONGA)

Xiluvana (f) The little flower. (XITSONGA)

Ximanga (m) The cat. (XITSONGA)

Ximbembe (m) The North wind. *Referring to someone who gets angry but soon calms down.* (XITSONGA)

Ximitantsengele (m) One who swallows a sour plum. *An expression used to name an adventurer.* (XITSONGA)

Xindulume (m) The rich one. (XITSONGA)

Xingwenya (m) The little crocodile. (XITSONGA)

Xinonwana (f) The little mouth. (XITSONGA)

Xintsundzuxo (m) Advice. (XITSONGA)

Xirhandziwa The beloved one. (XITSONGA)

Xirilela The one who weeps for it. (XITSONGA)

Xirilo The cause of tears. (XITSONGA)

Xi-sala-ndzhaku See 'Xi-sa-ndzaku'.

Xi-sa-ndzhaku The one who remains behind. *The mother died, the child lives.* (XITSONGA)

Xisiwana Poor. (XITSONGA)

Xisungulo Beginning of action. (XITSONGA)

Xithusamotoya One who threatens but does nothing. (XITSONGA)

Xitshembiso Xitsembiso (m) Assurance. (XITSONGA)

Xitsundzuxo (m) Advice. (XITSONGA)

Xitundulu (m) Person of good repute. (XITSONGA)

Xitundulume (m) Person of good reputation. (XITSONGA)

Xivambalana (f) The little dove. (XITSONGA)

Xiviri Essential body. (XITSONGA)

Xiviti (f) Bitterness. *A woman will name this child to express what she is feeling about her surrounding circumstances.* (XITSONGA)

Xivono (m) One who sees beyond the natural. (XITSONGA)

Xivula (m) The promised one. (XITSONGA)

Xiwutlanyana (m) The little chief. (XITSONGA)

Xola (m) Stay in Peace. *If there have been fights between the family members, the birth of a child can mark a point of reconciliation.* (NGUNI)

Xolani (m) Forgive. (NGUNI)

Xoleka Be quite satisfied. (NGUNI)

Xolela (m) See 'Xolani'.

Xolelo (m) Forgiveness. (NGUNI)

Xolelwa (f) Has been forgiven. (NGUNI)

Xolile Xoli (f) Has forgiven. (NGUNI)

Xolisa (f) Ask for forgiveness. (NGUNI)

Xolisile (f) Has asked for forgiveness. (NGUNI)

Xoliswa (f) Has pardoned. (NGUNI)

Xolo Harmony. (NGUNI)

Xongisa (f) Beautify. (XITSONGA)

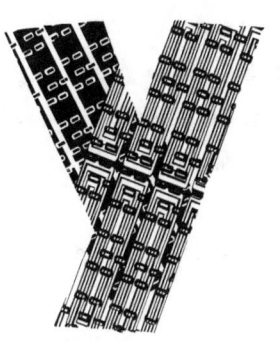

Yakhe Of him. (NGUNI)

Yanda Increase. (NGUNI)

Yandisa To add on. (NGUNI)

Yandiswa Be increased. (NGUNI)

Yanele Yanela Enough. (NGUNI)

Yanga May God. *The name 'yanga' means 'may'. It is extracted from the prayer expression: 'May God hear our prayers'.* (NGUNI)

Yazabantu (m) You must know people or have Ubuntu. (NGUNI)

Yedwa (m) Alone. (NGUNI)

Yedwana (m) Just alone. *This name is for a child without siblings.* (NGUNI)

Yenayena (m) The very one. (SOTHO)

Yethu Ours. (NGUNI)

Yihlo (m) Father. (NGUNI)

Yihlokazi (m) Paternal uncle. (NGUNI)

Yihlokhulu (m) Grandfather. (NGUNI)

Yingwana (m) The little leopard. *The tendency to use animal names is because of the behaviour, personality and certain character traits which the name-bearer is thought to share with a specific animal.* (XITSONGA)

Yinhle (f) The beautiful one. (NGUNI)

Yintle (f) See 'Yinhle'.

Yolanda (f) The go-getter. (NGUNI)

Yolela (f)   Be pleasant. (NGUNI)

Yolisa (f)   One giving pleasure to. (NGUNI)

Yoliswa (f)   To delight in. (NGUNI)

Yonayona (f)   The very one; authentic. (SOTHO)

Yondela (f)   Gaze at. (NGUNI)

Yonela (f)   Be satisfied. (NGUNI)

Zaba (m)   Resemblance. (NGUNI)

Zabalazile   The one who has tried hard. *After a difficult time trying to conceive.* (NGUNI)

Zabantu (f)   Belonging to the people. (NGUNI)

Zabo (f)   Theirs. (NGUNI)

Zakhelani (m)   Those who are building close to each other; neighbours. (NGUNI)

Zakhele (m)   Build for yourself. *Given to an independent child.* (NGUNI)

Zakhona (f)   Truly belonging to the family. (NGUNI)

Zakithi (f)   They belong to our family. (NGUNI)

Zalekile (f)   Causing fulfillment. (NGUNI)

Zalisekile (f)   *See 'Zalelike'.*

Zama   You must try. (NGUNI)

Zamadlomo (f)   Of the 'Dlomo' family. (NGUNI)

Zamageba (f)   Of the 'Zulu' Family. (NGUNI)

Zamahlubi (f)   Of 'Amahlubi' family. (NGUNI)

ZamaKhosi (f)   Of royalty. (NGUNI)

Zamambo (f)   Of the 'Mkhize' Family. (NGUNI)

Zamanene (f)   Daughter of the 'Nene' family. (NGUNI)

Zamani (m)   You must strive. (NGUNI)

ZamaQwabe (f)   Daughter of the 'Qwabe' Family. (NGUNI)

Zamaqwati (f)   Of the 'MaQwathi' family. (NGUNI)

Zamazulu (f)   Daughter of the 'Zulu' family. (NGUNI)

Zameka (f) Be improved; be better. (NGUNI)

Zami (f) Mine. (NGUNI)

Zamikhaya Persevere with the tasks of building a home. (NGUNI)

Zamile See 'Bazamile'. (NGUNI)

Zamiwani They have tried everything. (XITSONGA)

Zamokwakhe Zamo His or her effort. (NGUNI)

Zamuxolo Try to be at peace. (NGUNI)

Zamxaka The situation is now beyond control. (NGUNI)

Zandile Zandi (f) They have increased. (NGUNI)

Zandisiwe Zandisile (f) The girls have been increased. (NGUNI)

Zandiswa (f) They have been increased. (NGUNI)

Zanele Zenele (f) We have enough girls. (NGUNI)

Zanemvula The one who comes with the rain. *Name given for a child born on a rainy day.* (NGUNI)

Zanyiwe They have made an effort. (NGUNI)

Zazi Know yourself. (NGUNI)

Zaziwe Famous one. (NGUNI)

Zekhethelo (f) Belonging to a class of her own. (NGUNI)

Zenani Of great worth. (NGUNI)

Zenzele Do for self. (NGUNI)

Zenzile You have done it to yourself. *Sometimes the girls will not listen to the chastening of elders. When an unwanted pregnancy results, such a name is given to the child.* (NGUNI)

Zenzo (m) Deeds. (NGUNI)

Zesimanjemanje (f) The fashionable one. (NGUNI)

Zethembiso Promises. (NGUNI)

Zethu (f) Our girls. (NGUNI)

Zibekile Well-behaved one. (NGUNI)

Zibizetheku The dirt of Durban. *In this case, the mother gave her child this name when she had just discovered that her husband was having an extramarital affair with someone in Thekwini, Durban.* (NGUNI)

Zibonele See for yourself. *Name usually given to a girl who gives birth in her homestead and the parents are communicating that it is her responsibility to raise the child.* (NGUNI)

Zibongiwe (f) They have thanked. (NGUNI)

Zibulo (m) The first-born son. (NGUNI)

Zibuse (m) Be self-regulating. (NGUNI)

Zibusiso Blessings. (NGUNI)

Zibuyile (f) They have returned. *The birth of a child means that the maternal side has returned the cows used to pay the bride price.* (NGUNI)

Zifihlephi Where will you hide yourself? *Probably from shame or from the envious ones.* (NGUNI)

Zifikile (f) They have come. *The father had just handed over the cows for the lobola at the birth of the baby.* (NGUNI)

Zikhali (m) The equipped one. *This is also used as a surname.* (NGUNI)

Zikhona (f) The girls are here. (NGUNI)

Zikwepha (m) Hard work. (NGUNI)

Zilungile (f) They are good. (NGUNI)

Zimasa Support. (NGUNI)

Zimasile The one who is a supporting pillar. (NGUNI)

Zimbali (f) Flowers. (NGUNI)

Zimbili (f) They are two. *Used for twin girls.* (NGUNI)

Zimbini (f) They are two. *Used for twin girls.* (NGUNI)

Zimele Stand on your own. (NGUNI)

Zimisele Be purpose-driven. (NGUNI)

Zimkhitha Zimkitha (f) They are beautiful. (NGUNI)

Zindzi (f) The stable one. (NGUNI)

Zindzile (f) Well settled. (NGUNI)

Zine (f) They (the children) are four. (NGUNI)

Zingiso Zingisa Perseverance. (NGUNI)

Zinikele You must sacrifice yourself. *This name was used to encourage the mother in her new role.* (NGUNI)

Ziningi (f) There are many girls. (NGUNI)

Zinninzi (f) There are many girls. (NGUNI)

Zintathu (f)   They (the girls) are three. (NGUNI)
Zintle (f)   They (children) are beautiful. (NGUNI)
Zinyobulala   The only child in the family. (NGUNI)
Zinzi (f)   Be firm. (NGUNI)
Zinzile (f)   Steadfast. (NGUNI)
Zinzisile (f)   Have helped us get established. (NGUNI)
Ziphakanyiswa   The exalted one. (NGUNI)
Ziphelele   They are now complete. (NGUNI)
Ziphezinhle   Our lovely gifts. (NGUNI)
Zipho   Gifts. (NGUNI)
Ziphokuhle   Give yourself what is good. (NGUNI)
Ziphozethu   Our gifts. (NGUNI)
Ziphozonke   All the gifts. (NGUNI)
Ziqede (m)   Finish them up. *Name from the expression 'Qedi zindaba', meaning the one who knows them all. Usually said as a telling name for a gossipper within a society* (NGUNI)
Zithembe (m)   Have self-confidence. (NGUNI)
Zithulele (f)   Keep oneself quiet. *That was a response to a family dispute.* (NGUNI)
Zithulise (f)   Comfort yourself. *Usually said of someone who has been weeping. Names such as this can be given when there has been a situation causing sorrow in the home and the birth of a child can be regarded as a consolation.* (NGUNI)

Ziyanda (f) *See 'Ayanda'.*

Zizipho (f) They (children) are gifts. (NGUNI)

Zizwe (f) Nations. *The child might have been conceived outside the country of residence.* (NGUNI)

Zodidi (f) Of a certain kind or class. (NGUNI)

Zodumo Famous one. (NGUNI)

Zodwa (f) Alone. (NGUNI)

Zodwana (f) Only girls. (NGUNI)

Zokhethelo (f) Special one. (NGUNI)

Zokuthula (f) Belonging to peace. (NGUNI)

Zola Be calm. (NGUNI)

Zolani (m) Quietness. (NGUNI)

Zoleka The calm one. (NGUNI)

Zolekana The little calm one. (NGUNI)

Zolile *See 'Zolani'.* (NGUNI)

Zolisa (f) Cause calmness. (NGUNI)

Zoliswa (f) *See 'Zolani'.*

Zondelelile (f) A zealous one. (NGUNI)

Zondiwani (f) Someone who is disliked. (XITSONGA)

Zondlile (f) She has nourished herself. (NGUNI)

Zondwazi (f) The hated one. *Mother expressing that she is aware that they hate her, usually the in-laws.* (NGUNI)

Zonke All. (NGUNI)

Zonwabele (f) Celebrate. (NGUNI)

Zotha (f) Be humbled/ dignified. (NGUNI)

Zothile (f) Calm and humbled one. (NGUNI)

Zoxola (f) Belonging to forgiveness. (NGUNI)

Zubakazi (f) Well-dressed woman. (NGUNI)

Zukile Zuki Famous. (NGUNI)

Zukisa Make famous. (NGUNI)

Zukiswa Have received grace. (NGUNI)

Zuko The gracious one. (NGUNI)

Zukolwethu Our grace. (NGUNI)

Zumekile One who has been taken by surprise. (NGUNI)

Zungwana (f) Brass neck ring. *Part of the traditional dress for Ndebele women.* (NGUNI)

Zuzekile (f) We have obtained her; gained. (NGUNI)

Zuziwe (f) One who has been gained. (NGUNI)

Zwakele We have been heard. (NGUNI)

Zwakushiwo Hearsay. *People were telling the grandmother that the child was illegitimate.* (NGUNI)

Zwana Small child. (TSHIVENDA)

Zwanga Mine; that which belongs to me. (TSHIVENDA)

Zwelakhe (m) Own land. (NGUNI)

Zweledinga (m) The land of those in need. (NGUNI)

Zwelenduna (m) Headman's land. *The headman was contending that the land belonged to him.* (NGUNI)

Zwelenhlanhla (m) Fortunate land. (NGUNI)

Zwelethu (m) Our country. *Chiefs and royals sometimes will use names associated with the land to show their rule.* (NGUNI)

Zwelibanzi Zweli (m) The earth is wide enough. (NGUNI)

Zwelibuyile (m) Our land has been restored. (NGUNI)

Zwelihle (m) A beautiful land. (NGUNI)

Zwelikhethabantu (m) The earth chooses people. *Adapted from an expression which means someone has been favoured by nature.* (NGUNI)

Zwelinzima (m) The world is a hard place. (NGUNI)

Zwelisha (m) A new land. (NGUNI)

Zwelivelile (m) The land has appeared. (NGUNI)

Zweliyaduma (m) The land is making a sound. *It may be that a child was born when there were rumours of war.* (NGUNI)

Zwelo (m) Compassion. (NGUNI)

Zwi The only one we have. (NGUNI)

Zwidofhela (m) The bad treatment will come to an end. *The name refers to a situation where one might be ill-treated, and through this name the name-giver says that all the suffering will come to an end one day.* (TSHIVENDA)

Zwiito (m) Short form of 'Zwiitwaho'. (TSHIVENDA)

Zwiitwaho (m) Things that are done. *Usually talking of undesirable things.* (TSHIVENDA)

Zwithuzwavhudi (m) Good things. (TSHIVENDA)

Zwodangani (m) Who brought them? Or How did they come? *Such a name was used as a communication strategy to the in-laws who made a surprise visit.* (TSHIVENDA)

Zwoitea (m) It happened. *When something that has been waited for, finally happens.* (TSHIVENDA)

About the Author

Born in a small town of Piet Retief (eMkhondo), Phumzile Simelane Kalumba graduated from the University of Cape Town in 1998 with a BCom degree. She lived in the North East of England with her family for 7 years. While there, she developed interest in South African Bantu names. She then went on to do an MA in the Department of Xhosa, at the University of Western Cape with a special interest in onomastics, a part of African folklore. She graduated in 2014. She has published a number of academic papers on naming and is currently working on an MPhil at the University of Cape Town.

www.ingramcontent.com/pod-product-compliance
Lightning Source LLC
Chambersburg PA
CBHW061706300426
44115CB00014B/2580